Questions

The Judaic Law

Questions

A series of explorations by
William Corlett & John Moore

WILLIAM CORLETT

&

JOHN MOORE

The Judaic Law

HAMISH HAMILTON

LONDON

First published in Great Britain 1979 by
Hamish Hamilton Ltd., Garden House
57–59 Long Acre, London WC2E 9JZ

ISBN 0 241 10006 2

Printed in Great Britain by
Ebenezer Baylis and Son Ltd.
The Trinity Press, Worcester, and London

This book is one of a series.

The titles are *The Question of Religion*, *The Christ Story*, *The Hindu Sound*, *The Judaic Law*, *The Buddha Way* and *The Islamic Space*. The books were written in the order as listed, but this in no way implies any suggested precedence of one religion over another, nor any preference on the part of the authors. Each book may be read in its own right, rather as each note of an octave may sound alone.

However, for an octave to be complete, it depends on the developing frequency and character of each note. In the same way, it has been the experience of the authors, approaching this series as one work, to find a similar development as they progressed from one book to another.

And the Lord God said, Behold, the man is become as one of us, to know good and evil: and now, lest he put forth his hand, and take also of the tree of life, and eat, and live for ever:

Therefore the Lord God sent him forth from the garden of Eden, to till the ground from whence he was taken.

So he drove out the man; and he placed at the east of the garden of Eden Cherubims, and a flaming sword which turned every way, to keep the way of the tree of life.

(Genesis, 3:22–24)

One

This book, as with a religion, has to begin . . . somewhere in place and time.

How should we begin?

How does a religion begin?

Do we suppose that as someone may say, "Let's write a book", someone once said, "Let's start a religion and call it Judaism"?

However a religion (whatever "religion" *is*) may begin, must not its continuation depend on the viability or vitality of the idea, concept, experience—whatever it was founded upon—being relevant to the time, the place and the need?

Is a "religion" recognised as such at its beginning, or even during its gestation, or even during the first phase of its formalisation and growth towards maturity?

Can we find—and is there any point in finding—the beginning in time of a phenomenon such as a religion? Why are we so concerned with past history and the search for origins?

Would it in any way help us if we found the point in time when certain desert nomads said to themselves, "Let us found a religion . . ."?

Can the beginning ever be known . . . of an idea, concept, experience . . . which may later become manifest, be given a name or title and become formalised?

We look for the beginning of evolution by tracing back through our memories of the past.

We start this book by searching in memory. And you, the reader, may try to make sense of it by referring to your past learning and experience.

*

How and where does anything begin . . . including you and me?
How, where and when did *I* begin?

Perhaps we shall see as we proceed with this book that we are conditioned to believe in beginnings, continuings and endings by our concept of time . . . which is entirely based on the relative motions of bodies through space.

We can begin the exploration anywhere . . . and we may find that we are *bound* to end where we began . . . back at the beginning. The difference is that in between—in the mean-time—we may better understand the beginning.

Judaism tells of One (and is called a monotheistic religion). And it tells how that One gave rise to Everything . . . and how Everything must resolve back into One.

Its emphasis is not so much on "One God" as is commonly supposed; rather is it on "the Lord is One".

"Hear O Israel: The Lord our God, the Lord is One!"

*

It does not matter where we begin nor how we choose to express ourselves . . . so long as we speak of the nature of the Law . . . as it was proclaimed to Israel.

Creation cannot begin other than with and out of the One . . . and it is enough from the religious point of view if we understand and realise that it ends in One . . . otherwise its story . . . and our own story—is not whole and complete.

All the rest—the middle—is expression as to how the One governs all generations (through the "patriarchs") through the unfolding of time . . . and the inevitability through time of the return to One.

That is the Judaic Law . . . and it applies to this place, *here* . . . and this time, *now* . . .

Two

Now, at this moment, as I begin to write these words, I am at a point in time. Thus, from the moment of my birth to this moment *now*, a certain number of years have passed—a certain number of days, hours, minutes, seconds. I can say I am "such an age"; I say I am "so many years old".

I can be precise about this because TIME is meticulously measured. Thus, in any given day there are twenty-four hours; in each hour there are sixty minutes; and in each minute there are sixty seconds.

Who first measured a minute—and why?

Who first measured a second—and why?

Why are my hours marked by the hands of a clock?

Why are the days of my life ruled by the revolving of the earth?

Why is my life measured by the number of times I travel around the sun?

Such questions do not usually trouble me.

It is all something that I take for granted.

And I never question why time was "invented".

*

What I accept is that within the phenomenal world of my experience I have abundant evidence of time.

The sun rises in the east—and the dawn is my experience.

The sun travels through the sky above me (or so it seems)—and morning passes to high noon, and afternoon fades into evening. I witness it happening.

The sun sinks behind the horizon to the west—and darkness descends. I experience that day has "passed" and night has "come".

3

And because this process has taken place for as long as I remember, I do not wonder that it could ever be otherwise. I sleep peacefully, confident that there will be another dawn tomorrow . . . and another day.

Similarly, I am able to watch the seasons change from spring to summer to autumn and to winter. I see buds form on apparently dead twigs; and I see the buds swell and blossom and fruit and wither and die . . .

The cycles of the seasons and of the years continue in an ordered progress and I am always there to witness the changing.

*

Now . . . at this moment . . . as I write these words . . . I am at a point in time, on the frontier of time past and time future.

Already . . . the point I referred to in the line above was "earlier" . . . time has passed . . . the frontier has moved on.

I am a little older. Seconds have ticked away. The day is a little more advanced; the sun a little higher in the sky . . . *everything* in nature has changed. A bud is nearer breaking; a flower is about to die.

I am a little further from my birth and a little nearer to my death. I *pass over* a little more of my life.

Time is passing.

Passing who or what?

For it to be passing there must be that which it passes.

Life means change . . . ever-changing . . . always changing.

Is there any way of stopping this inexorable process of change, this inevitable growing and decaying, this waxing and waning?

No . . . it is the Law. It is lawful.

Life means change.

If there were no change, there would be no movement.

You and I would not be living.

*

Because I hold the belief in time passing, I have the concept of "time past" and "time future".

4

Here I am, now, writing these words.

Here you are, now, reading these words.

To my "now" of writing, your "now" of reading is in the future; and to your reading "now", my "now" of writing is in the past.

Are the two connected? How?

Just by the space of days, months, years?

*

I can "remember" some time ago beginning to write this book. I have "clear proof" that time has passed . . . how else did these words get written down on the page? It took "time" to write them. The hands have moved through several degrees on the face of the clock.

If I had written faster . . . by "now" I could have written some of the words that I haven't yet written!

Or, if I had written slower, these words that I am "now" writing would still be in the future!

So what is this phenomenon called TIME . . . this measuring of "lawful change"?

Or, to put it another way, I say "here I am now" . . . NOW! . . . how long is "now"?

Is NOW a second, a minute, an hour?

Of what duration is "the present moment"?

What is the time-space between one "now" and another "now"?

How is my "now" connected with your "now"?

How can the writer's "now" be the reader's "future"; and how can your reading "now" be my "past"?

*

PAST ←——————————←– NOW →————————→ FUTURE

Where is NOW on a historical, chronological line from the past into the future?

The only answer we can give is . . . "NOW"!

And of course such an answer depends on when we say "NOW"!

*

5

But as soon as we have said it, it is past.

As we are saying it, it is passing.

"It came to pass . . ."

As the mind concentrates towards the "split-second" that divides past from future, "now" is ever-elusive.

The tiniest fraction of a second slips *past*.

Could "now" be "no time at all"?

"Now" never passes.

*

The "laws of passing time" are concepts of mind, as it measures one thing moving in relation to another, separate thing.

The mind conceives of many such laws as it observes the experience of being in this world and learns its explanations.

And this book is about such laws and what arises from them. It is about the emphasis we place on them and how we live by them. And it is about how they perhaps delude us and put our nature in bondage.

And we will surely find that through not realising what we have believed, we are subject to more laws than we might at first think. We little realise how we came upon our view of the world.

*

There are what man has called "the natural laws of the universe".

There are the man-made laws pertaining to the society to which we happen to belong, designed to protect the society and its members.

And there are our own personal laws which have become established in our minds by our conditioning, by our reaction to our experience of life.

Some laws we quite naturally and happily obey, sometimes without ever thinking about them; and there are others which we question and perhaps find to be a burden, especially if we cannot understand the reason for them.

We may even defy and perhaps even break laws, rendering ourselves liable to punishment. And we have to cope with the fact that laws are changed—what was lawful yesterday may become unlawful today, and vice versa. New laws are created and old laws are abandoned.

Every single manifest form is regulated by law; and every single action is regulated by law, is performed within law, of one kind or another. Every single event is conditioned by law.

*

At the level of human society, certain members are entrusted with the power to make law; and others to see that the law is interpreted, obeyed, and if necessary enforced.

All this we take for granted.

But has it always been so?

And why is it necessary?

In an "ideal" society I can see that social laws and their enforcement would not be necessary because all men would naturally live for the good of the society as a whole. If there were no laws, there would be no law-breakers; and if there were no law-breakers, there would be no known law!

However, such a Golden Age seems very far removed as a possibility given the present state of our civilisation.

And, even then, we are only speaking here about the social laws of the tribe.

We would still be subject to the great, universal laws of nature.

The days and the years would still "pass".

That which is "born" would still "die"; there would still be growing and decaying.

Or ... in believing that and taking it so much for granted, might we have fallen totally into an extraordinary illusion?

What is law?

Where does it come from and why?

How did we come to know of it?

What is the purpose of it?

To *whom* or *what* does it apply?

*

Law defines possibilities.

The impossible is so because there is no law to govern it.

Law defines limits of change. The universal or natural laws dictate what our physical bodies are able or not able to do. Man-made laws define how we must or must not behave.

Why should we have these limits?

Why should there be boundaries to our possibilities?

Could it be that there is that in man which is not subject to law —something which is free of, or above, the law?

And, if so, would not one way of finding it be to study and understand the structure and limits of law itself?

*

For example, we have suggested that in our experience we have conceived of the notion "time". We have noted the cyclic motions of the earth and sun and we have learned of hours and years. And the measurement of movement has given us distance and space and from time and space and movement we have velocities, accelerations, frequencies, lifetimes and so on, and so on. A proliferation of "scientific law".

Do we believe it all? Why do we believe it?

Because in physical, pragmatic terms it can all be useful?

But what law governs NOW, for example?

If, as we have suggested, NOW is "no time at all", can it be subject to change?

And, if it is not subject to change, it cannot be defined or limited by "physical" laws as we understand them.

Could this be the sort of "chink" through which we could see "another world", "a promised land", a Zion, which is not subject to the laws of this world—one that we might call "timeless", "eternal", "unchanging"?

If, as we have suggested also, law governs everything in manifest existence, it follows that that which is above the law cannot itself be in manifest existence.

*

And the Lord God commanded the man, saying, Of every tree of the garden thou mayest freely eat:

But of the tree of the knowledge of good and evil, thou shalt not eat of it: for in the day that thou eatest thereof thou shalt surely die.

(Genesis, 2:16, 17)

*

If law governs every aspect and atom of our existence from birth to death, then we are *totally* subject to the duality of keeping or breaking the law—and upon this will depend our concept of good and evil.

What is "good"? What law defines it, absolutely?

When is "now"? What law defines it?

What is the "present" (the "pre-sent") moment?

How long is "a lifetime"? What law decrees the time to "die"?

How many heartbeats in a life? What scientific law states the number?

How "big" is space? What law limits its boundary?

Where . . . Who . . . What . . . is "God", the Lord, the Law-Giver?

Why do I live? What law decreed my birth?

What is the point of the universe if no one knows of its existence? Who am I?

The law governs everything about myself—what I can do and what I cannot do, what I must do and what I must not do.

But *I* observe that law . . . what governs Me?

*

In the first moments of life . . . those innocent first moments after birth . . . who was I?

Did I think; if so, what did I think about?

Did I have "knowledge of good and evil" when I was born?

Did I judge experience, as "lawful"?

Or did I simply experience?

9

In those first innocent moments, did I consciously judge experience "good" or "bad"?

Or was it simply *pure experience*?

*

It is difficult for us not to presume and pre-judge ... but let us for a moment try.

Let us put ourselves in the imagined state of being the newly-born babe that once we were.

Let us do this consciously. Let us *know* that we are doing it, here and now.

You have just been born.

Close your eyes ... wait for a few moments ... and then open them.

You are seeing the world for the very first time.

What happens?

*

Try it again.

Close your eyes ... wait for a few moments ... and then open them.

Do you know *where you are*?

*

Was there a moment, after opening the eyes, when you saw, let us call it "a panorama of unnamed shapes and colours" ... before, as it were, the eyes focused on particular objects?

*

Is there a moment when there is only total and simple "seeing" ... before there is the recognition of a familiar something?

What if it were the very first time you had ever seen such a sight?

What would it all be before you had learned the names of things and about their functions?

How would it be if none of it were recognisable and familiar?

That moment—before the total-everything becomes a multitude

of separate, recognisable things—we would call the innocent or "unknowing" state.

As soon as we start to learn about the world, we go straight through that state into a world where everything has become many things, all defined by names, numbers and properties.

*

Let us try something further.

Close your eyes and then scratch the nails of one hand across the palm of the other. Just that. Try it.

Close your eyes and do it.

How would you describe the sensation?

Pleasant or painful?

If we call it either, how do we know?

What we call "pleasant" or "painful" is surely relative?

To what?

Supposing you had just been born, would you *know* it as "pleasant" or "painful"?

We build our own judgement from remembered experience. No one but you knows where you divide the pleasant from the painful.

But each sense must once have been used for the first time; how do we judge the first experience?

Who experiences? And who judges?

And does not experience come before judgement?

*

We have called this book *The Judaic Law* and it is one of a series of books that began with *The Question of Religion*.

In this book we are going to attempt to obtain a flavour, *through our own experience*, of the Judaic faith-religion and its standpoint . . . what it is that the Judaic scriptures are saying to us, the authors.

Through such an exploration, we hope to learn more about man and the phenomenon of religion. But essentially, for it to be of any real value, such an exploration must teach us more about ourselves—what we think we are, what it means to understand the laws that govern us.

II

Thus, this is not a vicarious learning exercise about other men's experience in history, other men's beliefs, but a way for us to approach the deep and ancient mysteries of each and every life, through a testament first *written down* in Hebrew two thousand years ago.

We may not at the end be any the wiser about the complicated theology, ritual and ceremony that gives form and cohesion to a particular religion called Judaism; that is not the purpose of this book. But we may discover something vital about the function of all the laws which govern us and begin to understand how that function is not to bind us but show us what freedom means.

*

And perhaps this process has already begun.

We have spoken about the "*first*, pure experience" of our coming-to-be in this world, and about the "related or recognised experience" which quickly follows as soon as we have begun to learn about the world and to take our place in it.

Is it possible—or desirable—I wonder, to return to the innocent state of the first, clear, light, pure experience?

Could we—do we want to be—free of the laws that condition and rule our existence here on earth?

"Eden" is a Hebrew word meaning "delight". The Garden of Eden means literally "the enclosed place of delight".

It is a place, we are told, where man once belonged—and from which he was banished.

Why, if we interpret it historically, should we now, as mankind, continue to suffer banishment and have to "till the ground" as retribution for disobedience by "the first man and woman" (Adam and Eve) "many millennia ago" at the beginning of time?

Plainly, such a literal, historical approach is not going to help us at all. It can only lead into blind speculation and absurdities.

But what is it *really* suggesting to us, *now*?

It may just be a primitive myth—but why does it touch something very deep within?

Why, in particular, does it seem plausible to think that maybe life and living as we come to find it in this world is not all there is to it? Do we just come into existence to learn about things, to work, to seek pleasure, to avoid pain, to fight, to love, to hate, to enjoy fleeting moments, to procreate, to decay and disintegrate? Is that *really* all there is to it?

Or is there a way through which we may return to a quite-other "life" in a quite-other "place"?

Perhaps we *have*, all of us, mankind collectively, been "banished" and we have somehow to "earn"—or make ourselves fit for—a "return to Eden"?

In that question we have the basic Judaic desire and motivation —the yearning for the "Promised Land".

And we, be we "Jewish" or not, can all *feel* that yearning.

In that yearning, we all *feel* the urge to examine the nature of our "bondage" and look for the possibility of "freedom".

*

This process of examination has already begun . . .

We are not studying other people, their history nor how and why they perpetuate a particular performance of religious custom and belief. We, as mankind, whatever our tribe or conditioning, are studying ourselves, our behaviour, our deepest questions and longings.

And to do so, we should not be afraid to explore any teaching, any clue. Such teachings belong to mankind as a whole. In the era of "universality" into which we are now moving, all ideas of exclusivity and superiority are sure to be dispelled.

*

The scriptures we shall mainly consider and quote from are the first five books of the Hebrew Bible, sometimes called The Pentateuch and also called the Torah (the Law).

Here we will find the story of the beginning of the world, the creation of man, his fall and the generation of the children of Israel—how they grew and multiplied after their original parents

13

were banished from Eden; how they suffered hardship and vicissitude and came to believe that all their tribulations were a punishment from their "God"; how they were sold into slavery in Egypt, and how they rose up and escaped and set off on the long and perilous journey in search of the "Promised Land", where they could live in peace and harmony, having found favour "in the sight of God".

So what on earth, we may ask, has that got to do with *me*, now. What indeed!

*

I assume I was born.

At least, at some point I knew I was here in this world.

And I assume that I lived for a brief period in "innocence", experiencing everything for the first time. (Only now do I call it "a brief period"; did I know it as a duration at the time?) And I assume that I had no concept of "good" nor "evil"—at least I certainly do not remember such a concept.

Just how much do I remember of that "innocence"? After my assumed conception in the darkness of my mother's womb, when did I first realise the experience of being here?

Whatever the first memories and however far back, what would we say was their nature? In retrospect, would we say they were "blissful"?

Was it like one of those occasional moments when one is "transported" . . . by the scent of a flower, by a view of overwhelming beauty, by a sound or a touch that melts the heart? Do I remember then, in that "innocent" experience, a state that once was natural to me?

Or when I recall days when the sun always seemed to be shining, when the sky was always blue . . . it can't have been, can it? So why do I recall it like that? Is it a trick of memory or did I really once live in a paradise, a "garden of delight", a Garden of Eden?

*

But, more to the present point, did I know it to be so at the time? Evidently not . . . certainly not, if I was innocent.

14

Besides, for it to have been *known* as a "garden of delight" I would also have to have *known* a "garden of despair" with which to compare it . . . wouldn't I? And I had had no experience with which to judge the nature of where I was.

And yet . . . was there . . . is there . . . can I eventually find . . . such a garden?

*

As I grew older, I began to learn—to walk, to talk, to count, to read. I learned about the laws and properties of the world and my society. And every day I became more and more convinced that time was passing, that space existed and distance separated me from all the things of the world. I learned that in order to survive and communicate I had to be understood; and I learned that I had to work.

Did I ever question all this?

And if I did, did anyone suggest an alternative?

And as I was educated—"led out of" ignorance—I learned the names of things and what things did. I learned more and more of laws and properties and I became more and more engrossed in the phenomenal world.

I also learned to compete. If I did well, I would obtain reward; if I did badly, I would suffer and be deprived of privilege. And if I disobeyed the laws, I would be punished. I came to know of "good" and "evil".

And the world said that I was "growing up". I was certainly following the same process that my parents had gone through (and generation upon generation before them) and that my contemporaries were also going through.

And yet, despite layer upon layer of conditioning, there was still deep within an innocence. Even when I reached puberty and sexuality emerged in my maturing body, and I became "initiated" into adulthood, capable of taking part in the procreation of new life, there was still a core of my "being" that had not changed.

And it was to this inner core, perhaps deep in my "heart", that the stories of the Garden of Eden spoke.

Was it there in the remote beginning of time; is it possible to go "backwards" through time to find it again?

Where is it? Here on earth or in some other magic realm of space and time?

Is it possible to get there . . . in the future?

*

Let us look at the creation story, contained in the first book of the Pentateuch called "Genesis" (the "becoming", the "coming-to-be").

In the beginning God . . .

*

At a static point in time, suddenly . . . it began?

If so, the educated mind protests: "How can time suddenly begin?" "If there was a commencement at a point of time, what was before the beginning?"

The mind committed to chronological time cannot cope.

And yet . . . it does not say that. "In the beginning" . . . a continuous, ever-present, here-now beginning, without commencement or ending?

Where does NOW commence and end?

Is it not always beginning . . . now?

*

"God"?

"Who or what is 'God'?" the mind asks, committed to the learning that everything named has location, qualities and properties.

How can mind comprehend the origins of itself?

Could it be that though the mind has learned much about many things in the world, it has to be taught in quite another way to know "God"?

Why should mind be restricted to such concepts as time, space, name, location, dimension, qualities, properties and so on?

*

16

In the beginning God . . .
And the unmanifest creation stirs in the "womb" . . .
And God said, Let there be light: and there was light . . .
The "first day of creation" . . .
And God said, Let there be a firmament in the midst of the waters . . .
The "second day of creation" . . .
And God said, Let the waters under the heavens be gathered together unto one place, and let the dry land appear . . .
The "third day of creation" . . .
And God said, Let there be lights in the firmament of the heaven to divide . . .
The "fourth day of creation" . . .
And God said, Let the waters bring forth abundantly the moving creatures that have life . . .
The "fifth day of creation" . . .
And God said, Let us make man in our image, after our likeness . . .
The "sixth day of creation" . . .
And on the seventh day God ended his work which he had made . . .

*

Now we may take this story how we will . . . and each must do so according to his inclination and preference.

It may well contain many levels of meaning. It could be taken literally, or symbolically, or as an allegory. Or it could simply be a man-invented myth (and it is interesting to note that many early societies have a "creation story" not unlike this one).

But, however we consider it, how can it be relevant to our present lives? How can it be relevant to your experience of life and mine . . . NOW?

We are only concerned in this present book to hint at one way . . . a way that is relevant to the writers of this book . . . NOW.

*

And God saw every thing that he had made, and, behold, it was very good . . .

Three

So God created man in his own image . . .

And "then", "after the heavens and earth were finished . . .", after the six days of creation, including the *creation* of man, "God ended his work which he had made; and he rested on the seventh day . . ."

And yet, though they had been *made*, the plants were not in the earth and the herbs were not growing, for it had not rained and "there was not a man to till the ground" (Genesis, 2:5).

And so, ". . . the Lord God *formed* man of the dust of the ground and breathed into his nostrils the breath of life; and man became a living soul." (Genesis, 2:7).

"Created man in his own image . . ."

"Formed man of the dust of the ground . . ."

Created and then *formed*? Made but not yet living?

How can this be?

What a strange sequence . . . or is it supposed to be a sequence at all, in "time" . . . as we move from Chapter 1 to Chapter 2 and "God" becomes "Lord God"?

Plainly, for the logical, scientific mind, we have a conundrum here, a mystery.

Could it be that the scripture is incomplete or has suffered through misinterpretation and mistranslation through being handed down through thousands of years? (Not very likely. The scriptures have been carefully preserved since their origination and it has been, and is, a strict discipline that when being transferred to new scrolls, the original is faithfully copied, not "one jot nor tittle" being omitted or altered.)

So, is there significance in the apparent illogicality, the changes of title and verb, the apparent contradiction. Is the disconnection between the phrases and chapters deliberate?

Such questions have exercised the minds of men for centuries. And they will no doubt continue to do so. But as we have said, no matter how tempting it may have been (and may be now) to make it more plausible, more logical, more up-to-date and scientifically acceptable, the original has not been abandoned nor altered. Despite the passing centuries, and the reams of interpretation throughout history, every letter, every word, every sentence, is sacred.

On what grounds could anyone presume to "improve" it?

*

So, it is not for us to suggest that there is a single, undeniable and absolute explanation.

But it presents a challenge which anyone may accept.

It represents a formidable exercise for the mind, stretching it to the limits of its powers of comprehension.

But if we are not to idle away our lives comfortably cocooned by the familiar, is it not a worthy challenge . . . that somehow we might just discover in age-old wisdom something crucial and meaningful that illuminates our existence now?

And, again, theory alone will not help us, or anyone else; it must be related to our experience.

It does not matter what the most celebrated prophets, rabbis, wise men or kings have proclaimed . . . unless it reveals the truth to you and me.

One of the reasons, surely, that these "ancient" stories have survived for so long is that they have served as inspiration, and may yet serve as inspiration, to *any* man?

*

"Adam" means "man".

Could the *first* man have been born of woman?

The time-bound mind says, "Of course not. Otherwise he would not have been the first man . . ."

19

But, having said that, what can it then do?

How do you conceive of a commencement . . . when the mind is committed to continuity and the repetitive finite?

How far back in time will memory take us?

Is there a beginning in time? And beyond that . . . before the beginning?

How does it seem to us . . . NOW?

*

Who conceived of you?

Did you accidentally happen to be you?

It was before your experience in this life but, somewhere in the "past", do you suppose that, when your father and mother desired and copulated, they *knew* who they were creating—that it would be "you"?

They may have hoped at the time that a child would be conceived, but could they dictate or imagine that it would be "you" in particular? In what way could you be said to be "theirs"?

In the time of their desire, "you" were not yet created. The potential or unmanifest "you" was in their desire, but formless.

By their act, the potential for there being "you" became manifest.

There was a "before your time" and then a "beginning of your time".

"You" were brought from the "unknown" and entered the realm of your parents' desire. A new chapter began for "you" when their desire was transformed into a physical joining together and they provided the "seed" and the "ground" for "you" to become possible, to become manifest.

Still "you" do not know of these acts which are preparing the way for your existence.

Who prompted their desire?

Who devised the act of copulation to make "you" a possibility?

Who guided "you" through from "before your time" to the "beginning of your time"?

*

*. . . in the day that the Lord God made the earth and the heavens,
And every plant of the field before it was in the earth, and every herb
of the field before it grew . . .*

*

(Genesis 2: 4–5)

Yet "you" do not remember.

"You" do not remember the meeting of the sperm with the ovum in the darkness of the "waters" of the womb. "You" do not remember being "formed of the dust of the ground".

How did the sperm and the ovum "know" how to grow "you"? How did the embryo "know" how to form your body, your limbs, your head, your heart, your brain?

Perhaps, NOW, the story of Genesis is a little less of an ancient tale . . .?

*

Then "you" were born out of the waters of the womb and "you" emerged from darkness into light, and "you" were divided from your mother, and into your "nostrils" was "breathed the breath of life".

Were you now "you"?

Or were you just "half" your mother and "half" your father?

Do "you" remember?

Or were you still "innocent" . . . still not knowing you were "you"?

*

And the Lord God said, It is not good that the man should be alone; I will make him an help meet for him.

And out of the ground the Lord God formed every beast of the field, and every fowl of the air; and brought them unto Adam to see what he would call them: and whatsoever Adam called every living creature, that was the name thereof.

And Adam gave names to all cattle, and to the fowl of the air, and to every beast of the field; but for Adam there was not found an help meet for him.

And the Lord God caused a deep sleep to fall upon Adam, and he slept: and he took one of his ribs, and closed up the flesh instead thereof;

And the rib, which the Lord God had taken from man, made he a woman, and brought her unto the man.

And Adam said, This is now bone of my bones and flesh of my flesh: she shall be called Woman, because she was taken out of Man.

Therefore shall a man leave his father and his mother, and cleave unto his wife: and they shall be one flesh.

And they were both naked, the man and his wife, and were not ashamed . . .

(Genesis, 2: 18–25)

*

"You" came into this world; and you heard, and touched and saw, and tasted, and smelled the world.

And "you" began to give names to what you sensed. And "you" began to become familiar with your conception of the world around you.

At first, "you" accepted totally. The sense impressions came into your consciousness and "you" experienced them, and reacted to them. And things were what "you" called them.

But did "you" have a sense of yourself . . . as being separate from the world about you?

Did "you" know yourself to be a separate and individual entity?

"You" were at one with the world?

Alone . . . al-one . . . all one?

*

But then . . . "you" began . . . to become aware of yourself . . . as a separate entity.

"*You" became aware of "yourself"*.

Who was aware of whom?

In the "deep sleep" of unified innocence, "yourself" was taken out of "you".

There was "you", the unknowing witness or being, and now

"yourself" as well . . . "the flesh and bone" (which unknowingly had been "within you" but was now projected out of "you" as the body-identified self, the "public person" taking a place in the world).

There was "I"—the central core of being—and the publicly identifiable person "me" which "I" had given life to—and continue to do so throughout the body's lifetime.

And so I began to know myself to be . . . *I came to be* . . .

And I began to know about myself . . . to think, to imagine, to remember, to "talk to myself", to dream about "me".

"I" was no longer alone.

"I" was divided and became two—the "male" spirit of my innocent being, and the "female" person, the "me" formed in the matter and image of my body.

"I" had "an help meet" . . . that through which "I" was enabled to meet and know myself.

Now I began to be other than just the product, the offspring, of my father and mother.

And I began to become me.

And I began to realise myself to be in my own time and in my own place.

And I "cleaved unto" this "partner" who had appeared in my mind.

And still "we" were innocent . . . the two-in-one that "I" became.

"We" were of the "one flesh" and were not hidden from each other.

There was nothing "I" and "me" were guilty of in that garden of childhood. We were as one as we ate of the fruits of that childhood world.

*

And then another "chapter" began in my life . . . as it does in Genesis.

I enjoyed the garden of my innocence and enjoyed the fruits of my existence; but I was not destined to remain there.

23

Out of my own private world, I came to become more and more aware of the so-called "real world out there".

More and more I became tempted into thinking and believing that I was the body in which I existed and which was steadily and inexorably growing towards maturity. I learned the names and properties of the "things" of the world and I, as the existing body-entity, was given a name.

And to that name I learned to respond.

And I learned to prefer the pleasurable to the painful.

And I began to desire and pursue the "things" of the world.

And thus I forgot "the beginning".

I—or rather, the body-identified "me"—entered the time and space of the physical world and the duality of what "me" wanted and did not want.

I began to "remember" a past and "imagine" a future.

I surrendered my "innocence" and absorbed "knowledge of the world".

And in so doing, I "forgot" the realms of my genesis.

*

And what happened to the "I"—the "first Adam" (who was *never* called by "the Lord God" by that name in the Garden of Eden)?

The "first I" of innocent being was forsaken. The identity was transferred. "I" became the body-identified being, as the power of this body in the world usurped my innocence.

"I" was now in the world—"I" and "me" together . . . Adam with Eve . . . spirit in matter.

"I" the pretender forgot the real "I" . . . and the pretender came to speak in my name.

"I" became "I am". I mattered.

*

And so we can continue to read the story—which the Christian has called "the Old Testament" . . . how "it came to pass", how it is that I am here and now in this world.

24

Certainly it is not the only interpretation of the story . . . and that is the richness and power of the most sacred stories told by man.

For example, we shall look at a more immediate experience of genesis in the next chapter of this book—a genesis that takes place "now", one that can be experienced "a hundred times a day".

For the ultimate hope and message of Judaism—as with all the great religions of the world—is that we are not "doomed forever" by our "fall" from innocence. On the contrary, though we are considering a difficult and perilous process, we may perhaps understand that it has a purpose. It is an inevitable process in the "divine plan" as we experience life and the world. And this process could not be fulfilled if we were not "born into this world".

*

We continue to read the story . . . we continue to grow older . . . perhaps we can begin to see that we actually are "living" the story . . . it is a "living story".

We may see whether the "prophecies" foretold in these stories are borne out in experience.

We may begin to realise, to "remember", how it "came to pass".

*

After the first years of innocence, we begin to view the world differently . . .

That which had been a "garden" in which "we have delighted to play" begins to become a restricted area, out of which we seek to break.

Our parents, who have been our guardians, our instructors, our mentors, our "law-givers", cease to hold quite such a dominance over us.

We seek friends of our own persuasions—with whom we may express and share our own, gradually-forming "personality"— our desires, our anxieties, our sorrows, our hopes, our fears.

Certain simple laws (or rules) that we were given in our infancy we now break. This is a vital moment. We are beginning to reject what in our innocence we never questioned and to seek for a set of values of our own.

We question a lot.

"Why?" we ask. "Why? . . . Why? . . . Why?"

"Why can't I do such and such?"

We begin to test ourselves against the world—to be "as a god".

"Why can't I eat the fruit from that tree?"

Is it sufficient simply to be told, "Because it is not allowed"?

No. We want to discover the answers for ourselves.

*

This process may be seen as the "loss of innocence"—and as such, it may be mistakenly regretted. For in regretting the "loss of innocence" we are "remembering the past". We are not here NOW.

And if we are not here NOW, how can we see what our present state is?

Why regret that which we have "lost" if we did not "know" we had it at the time?

For what was the real nature of that "innocence"?

What is innocence?

What can it mean for us?

Do we know?

Can it be measured, weighed, quantified?

For there to have been "known" innocence, would there not also have had to have been its opposite . . . should we call it "guilt"?

*

And Adam and his wife hid themselves from the presence of the Lord God amongst the trees of the garden.

And the Lord God called unto Adam, and said unto him, Where art thou?

(Genesis, 3: 8,9)

*

26

Where are YOU?
Are "you" hiding?
Do you hide from the "presence" NOW?

*

*And (Adam) said, I heard thy voice in the garden, and I was
afraid, because I was naked; and I hid myself.*

*

Do we hide from the truth?
Who are "you"?
Who am I?
Who is ashamed?
Who feels guilt?
I do.
Only *I know* the *feeling* of guilt . . . no one else can *feel* it for me.
I find myself guilty when I have "hidden" within myself that
I have broken the law.
And if, as in the Judaic faith, I have broken the Law of the
Lord God, then indeed I might well fear His "wrath".

*

We will discover that the Judaic Law is long and complicated.
It is as long and complicated, and as far-reaching and all-embracing,
as a lifetime spent outside Eden, cut off from our garden of delight
where we long to be . . . "some time".

We must *feel* the meaning of this book . . . for one *feels* happiness
or sorrow . . . there is nothing theoretical about it. (The intellect
may provide a logical explanation as to why it is being felt . . .
but that is a different world compared with the actual feeling
itself.) For one *feels* innocent, guilty, fearful, forgiven, hopeful . . .

Perhaps, when we question and investigate the laws, we will
discover that they are made to be broken—or rather, that once
we are truly lawful, they no longer constrict us, and we are free
within them.

But, again . . .

Who is it who was "once" innocent and is now "guilty"?
Who eats of the fruit of the knowledge of good and evil?
Why was the tree there?
Why was Adam forbidden to eat of it?
What was it for? As a catch for Adam? Why?

The Genesis story is our living experience . . . *our* story . . . *if we could but see and read it.*

That must be the hint of this book.

If for you, the reader, it is meaningless or pointless, forget it. If it accords with what you have already suspected or looked for, or are already finding, fair enough.

If it is enough for you that religion should be a performance of ritual, and belief that "somewhere" there is a "god", there is no point in exploring in this way.

But then, what is the point of religion . . . if it does not inspire, inform and, above all, reveal . . . what man's purpose is, what his responsibility is, what a religious life really means and, ultimately, how he may understand and know "God"?

*

In the first years of life, in a strictly "orthodox" Jewish family, the child is thoroughly indoctrinated with the Law and the Scriptures as they have been handed down for generations. Not only does he or she hear it in the synagogue, but religious ceremony and discipline is an integral part of home life, the special responsibility of the mother of the family.

Why such inculcation of doctrine?
To ensure salvation?
To avoid the fearful consequences of going astray?
The "carrot" or the "stick"?

*

Who is this "Lord God" who calls the tune?
We have "a long way to go" and we do not know "how much time we have"—and as it is a way of feeling we may require certain allowance and support for the journey.

28

We, the writers, can only speak from our point in the process . . .
and we crave, from ourselves, and from you:

Patience—for feelings are hard to express:

Honesty—for what we are looking at is ourselves:

Humour—the essential leavener in all "matters serious":

Single-mindedness—for we do not want to know what a Jew,
or anyone else, may think; we want rather, with the aid of Judaic
thought, to know . . .

Who am I?

*

The journey, after we leave the Garden of Eden, is through the
trials and wilderness of this world, in search of the Promised Land,
where we may dwell in peace and realise our true nature.

Surely all of us, "deep in the heart", want that?

So, why did we ever disobey "the Lord God"?

Why did we eat of the tree forbidden to us and condemn ourselves
"to die"?

*

*"A man is not honest simply because he never had the chance to
steal."*

(A Jewish folk saying)

Four

There was *a time* when I did not exist on this earth as "me".

There was *a time* when you did not exist on this earth as "you".

Such *a time* we call "before birth".

There will be *a time* when I will cease to exist on this earth as "me".

There will be *a time* when you will cease to exist on this earth as "you".

Such a time we call "after death".

From this we conclude that our existence is "between birth and death" . . . at least, this is how we are led to think and believe . . .

BIRTH→——————— EXISTENCE ———————←DEATH

However . . . did I exist a minute ago?

"Of course, I did," I will declare.

How do I know that?

"Because I remember doing so."

What *is* remembering?

Remembering . . . re-membering . . . "putting together again" . . . re-creating . . .

Be honest . . . what is it exactly that is being remembered?

*

Who is doing the remembering?

I am . . .

And who is remembered?

"I am", I will say. But can I be remembered, re-membered, in the past?

When is the remembering done?

Now.

And what do I remember?

A "previous now"? Do I really remember a "now that was"?

How can I possibly remember a "past now"?

I am . . . NOW.

*

Let us try it another way.

Is the "I" who is now remembering the same "I" who is being remembered?

The "I" who is now remembering is the "I" who *now is*.

But I am not "then" . . . I am now . . . I am remembering now . . . so how can I exist in the past?

"I am" always was, always is, and always will be, NOW.

*

What I remember now is a "scene" which was once witnessed.

What I remember is a past image of "me" . . . a view that was seen, a sound that was heard, a sensation that was felt, a feeling that was experienced, a thought that was formed, a dream that was dreamed . . . and because I identify myself with that past image I vaguely *think* now that somehow that is what I was.

But what has really happened?

Certainly the "vehicles" of that past experience—this body that I call "mine" and this mind that I call "mine"—have changed in the historical time that has passed. This body is a little older than it was—it may be a little taller, a little fatter . . . And this mind may have acquired a little more information, changed its belief or attitude a little . . . These experiences and changes happen to "me", the existing person.

But the "I", the witness of that experience and change, who was "there then" is here now. "I" am witnessing the remembering of "me". That "I" never changes . . . *is* only here and now . . . and cannot be remembered in time past.

I can recall past images and experience . . . but I cannot recall that which is always in the present . . . the "I am that I am".

*

I remember . . . yesterday, last week, a year ago . . . or rather, to be more accurate, I remember certain vague images from time past . . . a few memorable "nows" . . . when I was conscious of what was being experienced in the moment. I remember more or less vividly or vaguely . . . curious and odd details and emotions; but much of the total memory of that time is forgotten.

What fraction of the total possibility of a moment do I remember?

How many "nows" make a minute?

How many "nows" make a year?

How many "nows" make a lifetime?

How many of the "nows" do I fully live?

What is going on? Why do I remember so little . . . and forget so much?

*

If I am really honest, I remember certain "nows" . . . and then I have to locate them in historical time and say that it happened last week, or last year, or so many years ago.

And from that I assume that *I am continuous*.

Is that really a valid assumption?

Where was I during the "times forgotten"?

My body may continue a certain number of years in historical time and my mind may maintain more or less consistent beliefs, attitudes and opinions . . . but, am "I" continuous?

For instance, where am "I" when mind is "asleep"?

*

Having made the assumption that I am continuous (as long as the body lives and the mind is functioning "normally"), I say, "Of course I remember being alive a few moments ago. How else can I explain being here now?"

And I assume that I "have" time, can "make" time, can "take" time, can "save" time, can "give" time.

What, in heaven's name, am I saying?

*

Let us hypothesise again.

Sitting quietly, let us imagine for a moment that our memory has completely gone.

If I have no *memory*, then what is that "thing" in front of me?

Only memory tells me that it is a table.

What is it for?

Only memory tells me that it is to put things on.

If I have no *memory*, then where am I?

Only memory tells me that I am at home.

And what is home?

Only memory tells me that it is the place where I live and belong.

But, let us push a little deeper.

If I have *no memory*, then will I *ask* what the "thing" is in front of me (the table)?

If I have *no memory*, then will I *ask* where I am (at home)?

Without *memory*, would there be any question at all?

Do I, in fact, *remember* to ask the question, "What is that thing in front of me?"

If I have *no memory*, then is there not just a "thing" in front of me?

Is it not only *memory* that suggests that the "thing" is "some particular thing" (as opposed to "some other thing")?

With patience, we may discover that this is not quite such a futile enquiry as it may at first seem, for we are looking at how man "creates" his world, and lives his own "genesis".

Let us accept that we take the capacity to remember very much for granted—without realising what we are doing nor what the remembering *is doing to us*.

*

Who is doing the remembering?

What is this remembering?

"Established" memory is very quick.

I look and I see a "table". Memory works so quickly that I do not even realise that I have remembered the fact; I am not even aware that any "work" was involved. With the seeing, the recognition (the "re-knowing" of the fact) is "instantaneous". Unless, of course . . .

What if I have never seen the object before?

What if I have never before experienced the object that I am looking at?

What happens then?

I have no pre-knowledge of it, cannot re-cognise it, because I have no memory of it. What can I name it to myself then? And, if I cannot name it . . . then what is it?

To *me*, is it *any* thing?

It is made and formed . . . but to what extent is it created, for *me*? What is it before I believe it to be "some particular thing"?

*

Obviously, as of this moment, we are assuming a situation where "I" am *alone* (like Adam)—and thus not relying upon someone else giving me the benefit of their experience and learning, and hence *telling* me what the thing *is*. (And again, later, we may discover that this relationship of others to me is important in our enquiry into the Judaic faith-religion and, more specifically, into the Judaic Law.)

I am looking at something that in my knowledge I have never seen before.

What *is* that thing?

That it *is*, I cannot question.

But, is it enough that it *is*?

Am I not anxious to establish *what it is or does, in relation to me*?

And if I have no memory of its function, what alternative do I have?

Must I not discover what it is (and what it does) and, giving it a name, commit that name to memory?

Who gives it its name?

*

And out of the ground the Lord God formed every beast of the field

34

. . . and whatsoever Adam called every living creature that was the name thereof.

*

Before we understand the function of something, and before we have agreed to give it a certain name, it *is*, in isolation.

After we have understood the function, and each of us have given it the same name, it is some special "thing" in relation to us.

Thus electricity always *was*—but only became "electricity" when men "discovered" it and named it. Penicillin, the wheel, the atom . . . all the "discoveries" of man down through the ages always *were*, in *potential*, waiting to become manifest and, undertood and being named, to be used.

And the more the discoveries have accumulated, the more we say man has "progressed"?

In the same way, as each of us grows from babyhood through childhood, into adulthood, we accumulate understanding and names about more and more things in relation to us. And it is said that we are growing up, becoming more knowledgeable . . .

But in what respect?

Is this *really* so?

Does all the learning I have acquired make any difference to my understanding my being here *now*?

Did *I* learn to live?

Do *I* remember to go on living, day after day?

Do *I* remember to breathe, to make my heart beat?

Did *I* learn how to think or how to remember?

When I was first born, did *I* ask "Who am I?"

How does it come about that I should ask myself such a thing?

Can I remember . . . or do I have to be told?

And does all the learning add or detract one iota from the experience of being?

*

I learn to call a certain object a "table".

Would it matter if I had learned to call it an "elbat"?

And if someone who had never seen one before was to ask me, "What is that?", would I not answer with certainty, "It is a table"?

But is that what it *is* . . . or just what I have learned to call it?

I believe that that is what it is and, as I was led into believing it, so may I lead someone else into believing it.

But is what we call it, what it is?

*

Let us repeat our earlier exercises slightly differently.

Close your eyes. Let your mind become "empty" and quiet. And then open your eyes, imagining that you have completely lost your memory.

What do you see?

A panorama of shapes and colours, nothing named, nothing "known".

And now . . . something takes your attention . . . and meaning enters.

*

In so simple an exercise, there is such significance . . . and it happens so often and so quickly that we do not notice.

For example, every time you open your eyes after you blink, the visual world is "re-created". If you closed your eyes and never opened them again—if you suddenly went blind—where will the visual world have gone?

Or, again, have you noticed that you cannot give your attention to something that is not already there? No matter how quickly you look, or listen, or touch, or taste, or smell . . . can you see, hear, touch, taste or smell something *unless it is already there*?

And if it is already there, must it not already be made and formed *before* you are aware of it? Therefore, as far as the immediate NOW is concerned, does it not belong to the "past"?

Or perhaps we are witnessing the past "entering the present"?

"Before the beginning, there is only the desire to create . . ."

"In the beginning—the ever-present beginning—all things are created . . . given form and function."

36

And then they are given name . . . and man "creates" his own world, eastward of Eden.

*

Who am I?
"You are Adam."
Who said so?
Am I this form, this function and this name that it is *said* I am?

*

So far we have dealt with memory related to "things"
What about memory related to "events"?
As "things" are seen in *relationship* to us, so "events" *happen* to us.
"Events" *take place*, and they only have meaning in my experience if I am there to witness them—if they happen to "me".
How do I remember past events?
How do I call them to mind?
And, in calling them to mind, what happens to me *now*?

*

Again, let us try an experiment.
Can you remember getting up this morning?
Try. Remember getting up this morning.
Did you have a picture of yourself getting out of bed . . . as though you were watching somebody else?
Can you remember each moment, as it happened, from the moment of waking?
If so, it will take you as long to do so as it took to do it this morning!
But it isn't like that, is it?
In remembering getting up this morning, I seem to contract the whole experience into a single "memory" . . . the whole process of "getting up" is condensed in mind into a single "experience-thought".
I cannot remember myself being asleep ("before the beginning").

37

Nor can I remember the moment of waking up ("in the beginning").

But I can vaguely remember after I woke up . . . in this particular case, a simultaneous recalling of what at the time was a series of insignificant events. All at once, I remember that I knew I had to get up, that there were things to be done, that I did not want to leave the warmth of the bed, that consequently I did not get up at the moment I intended to . . . and so on . . . and so on . . .

I see a kind of "timeless cross-section" of the event . . . like a dream. I do not remember a continuous sequence—the movement of it. It is like a series of snap-shots.

What am I remembering?

Me? An earlier me? A younger me? What happened *to* me?

How long ago did it happen?

The clock would suggest a certain number of hours ago . . . but does it seem like that really? Was there awareness of continuous duration in between?

Certainly the mind will account for the time in between . . . by remembering that I did this and I did that . . . but does that really account for the duration? Can we ever experience a duration of time?

What is it that I am remembering and why do I remember certain random "snap-shots"? Why can we re-call what we have at present forgotten?

The further back in time that we probe, the more evident it becomes that we invent "continuity", that it is some kind of trick of the mind, an illusion. We could say that it is a bit like the operation of a cine-film, which is made up of a series of still pictures. It is only when these separate and discreet images are passed at a certain speed past a projector light that an illusion of movement is created on a screen; otherwise, each frame or image is only a motionless form.

This analogy can be analysed and compared with the human sight experience to very good effect and is very illuminating (as can that, say, of tape recording and sound, which again, depends on discreet signals passing a magnetic head at a certain speed in order to give a meaningful sound). We cannot pursue the analogy here but would we not say that our sense of passing time, continuity and movement entirely depends on the speed of succeeding impressions as they pass through the visual and auditory mechanisms "in the light of our present awareness, or consciousness, NOW"?

Why do we remember such apparently random and inconsequential "still pictures" of past scenes . . . sometimes strange and clear details . . . well "focused" as it were?

Why should I remember certain things easily and have forgotten others? Can I will myself to remember any moment of my past experience? What causes "forgotten" memories to jump into mind as if they are "asking" to be remembered? Could it be that every moment of my life is stored, latent, like films in cans or books on shelves, but I do not have the power, or there is no cause, for me to "re-member" them?

*

Perhaps the ability to recall them is connected with the power of the original experience? Perhaps, say, to the extent that the experience was stimulating, so that it "woke me up" and brought me into the present so that I was strongly aware of it?

Events, we have said, happen *to* us. *I* have to be there to witness the event in order that I may later be able to recall it. Perhaps, to touch again the analogy above, according to the degree to which I am conscious of the present so the power of the "projector light" and the accuracy of the "focus"?

If "I am not present", no light, no impression, no memory.

I have to be here *now*, in order that some time in the future I will be able to recall this moment . . . if I want to remember it, if it is worth remembering.

*

"But," you might say, "one is always here." Where else can one be?

Is this true?

What does it mean—to be here now?

39

My body is here, sitting at this desk. It is always here when I am . . . there is no denying that.

But my body doesn't do the remembering, does it?

What remembers?

My mind?

Is my mind always where my body is?

Where is "mind"? . . . What is "mind"? . . . In my head? . . . An instrument with the capacity to "remember"?

When the past is remembered, it is as if I use the mind, or the mind takes me, into another "realm" where the "past" can be seen, where an event can be touched again, "dead" though it may be.

While this takes place, however, I rely on the fact that my body remains in the present! Fortunately, I presume, my body does not go romping off into the past, to when it was younger! It stays in its own time.

*

The body is here now . . . and *I* know it to be, when *I* am here now.

Could I be here now if my body was not here now?

That is a leading question! But, confining our enquiry to ordinary, everyday experience, I would say that if my body were not here then neither would I be.

Or, to put it another way, it is by virtue of having a body that I am in this world, and am able to be aware of it.

And by virtue of having this body and mind, the question arises, "Who am I"?

The question is only asked in the present . . . NOW.

It cannot be asked when the mind is "dreaming" in the past or "imagining" in the future . . . only when I am in the body here and now.

And for the question to arise at all there must be a memory that there is an answer—to be remembered.

*

So, what have we got here?

It seems that ordinarily we have access to two "realms" at least and in those two realms two different orders of Law are operating.

The Law of the body—in the physical world—which is a fixed progression through passing time from birth to death, only existing, as far as *I* am concerned, when *I* am here now.

And the Law of the mind, not bound to the passing time of the physical world, able to recreate "me" in the realms of past and future.

This ability of the mind to "leave the present world" gives rise to much of the complexity and confusion that we can associate with human development. It is both the means of man's downfall and his fulfilment.

For where do *I* fit into this picture?

Am *I* bound to the limitations of the realms of body and mind?

Do *I* belong to yet another realm, a "third" world?

This essential core of my being, this Self, this spirit . . . who witnesses the body and the activities of the mind . . . where does it come from? . . . what is it? . . . where is it? . . . is it "bound" . . . to time . . . to place . . . to anything?

*

In simple terms, what we are saying is that body and mind are subject to two distinctly different orders of law, especially in relation to time and space.

The body's law—what we might call physical law—is scientifically measurable, is well defined and fixed, and is largely predictable. Its limits can be summed up in the statement:

"That which is born is bound to die."

Thus, if we could imagine a "mindless" body, and that body was fed and succoured, we could watch that body go through all the stages of life between birth and death.

"Mindless", the body's bio-chemical processes would simply continue for their allotted time.

Such a body could be called "innocent". It would only react to stimuli for, not knowing anything, it could not consciously will

41

or initiate any action. "Things" would happen to it; it would never judge them "good" or "evil". It would never make anything outside itself and would not take anything (other than the sustenance required to maintain it as a living organism).

What a long way this seems from what we call "living".

And yet, is this not the "innocent state" of the newly-born baby . . . which is how each of us once was? It is how it began for each one of us.

When we were born, "things" happened to us. Consider the very event of birth itself. What a staggering experience it must have been to find ourselves forced out of the warm, protective "shell" of the womb. How extraordinary it must have been to feel air on the skin for the first time . . . to hear sounds, without the muffling of our mothers' flesh . . . to breathe, for the first time . . . to see light, for the first time . . .

Is that when "my" independent mind began . . . with the first, independent breath?

At any rate, I assume that is when my independent mind began to function . . . a *pure mind* . . . an *innocent mind*.

Why do I call it that?

Because it had no remembered experience of this world with which to relate.

It was registering experiences of this world for the first time.

And such experiences!

Why do we not remember them now?

Was "I" there at the time?

*

Could it be that the experiences at birth (and possibly those during the later stages of gestation in the womb) established the primal pattern or blueprint through which we have moulded every experience since that time?

Could it be that since that "in the beginning" every event that has happened *to* the body, and has been evaluated *in* the mind, has been related back to that birth experience?

Perhaps the "emotional waves" spreading out through the

42

psyche from the shock of birth travel on to the moment of death?

*

So, we do not remember . . . whether we wanted or did not want to be born.

But, from the moment of birth, our historical time began . . . and inevitably we began to travel towards the moment of death.

The body comes into the world of physical time and space and the mind (wherever it came from and whatever it *is*!) begins to register experience, and the memory (whatever that *is*!) begins to record memories. And this process continues until death.

Each registering experience is compared with past experience . . . in the vague time of our history.

Some experiences we judge to be "pleasant"; they make us feel secure, comfortable, soothed, and so on.

Other experiences we judge to be "unpleasant"; they make us feel threatened, frightened, vulnerable, and so on.

In other words, each experience is evaluated. We judge it to be either "good" or "evil" from our point of view, *now* (that is to say, at the moment we are actually experiencing).

But "good" or "evil" in relation to what? In relation to when? *To the past.*

We relate experience back to the past . . . to a past sometimes so remote that we do not even consciously remember it . . . perhaps right back to a time when we lay helpless and innocent in our mothers' arms . . . only moments after experiencing the stupendous shock of birth.

*

We may not know where we are going, we say; but we do think we know where we have come from.

We may not know what will happen to us; but we can *remember* something of what has happened to us.

Our memory of the past moulds our judgement of the present.

As such, it could be said that we are "slaves" to that memory . . . as if we have been "sold into slavery".

43

So involved do we become in judging what is happening in the light of past experience . . . in order to promote the so-called "good" for us and to avoid the so-called "evil" . . . to manoeuvre to our advantage . . . that we "pre-judge" the experience and begin to fail to experience it "as if for the first time".

This being the case, "life" gradually begins to take on a repetitive and monotonous quality. "Things" happen with a sameness, a vagueness and a dimness. The more the mind is involved in interpreting the situation in relation to the past, the more there is a "dullness" about life . . . and the "faster" time seems to pass.

Then we begin to hope for a better tomorrow.

We begin to dream about the "future" . . . and to imagine what it will bring.

The power of the dream-future is as strong as the power of the past-memory.

And both the memory and the dream take us away from being here *now*.

*

So, where am "I" whilst all this is going on?
When and where did "I" begin?
With the first thing remembered?

*

And they heard the voice of the Lord God walking in the garden in the cool of the day; and Adam and his wife hid themselves from the presence of the Lord God amongst the trees of the garden.

And the Lord God called unto Adam, and said unto him, Where art thou?

And he said, I heard thy voice in the garden, and I was afraid, because I was naked, and I hid myself.

And he said, Who told thee that thou wast naked? Hast thou eaten of the tree, whereof I commanded thee that thou shouldest not eat?

(Genesis, 3: 8–11)

Five

There will be a time when I will cease to exist; there will be a time when you will cease to exist. Such a time is called "after death".

It is also a time "in the future".

The difference between time-past and time-future is very considerable for one simple reason:

Time-past is traced through memory and measured in historical duration; time-future is without known data or measurement.

Thus from the day my body was born until the present moment so many years have passed . . . so many months, weeks, days, hours, minutes, seconds . . . a duration . . . a fact supported by memory which remembers and "locates" particular events in chronological order.

But from the present moment to the time of the death of my body—in presumed time-future—there is no such "certainty" nor measurable duration.

I could die many years from now . . . or many months, or many weeks, or a number of days, or a few hours, in a few minutes, within the next few seconds . . . the moment may be right in front of me . . . I do not know where this inevitable event is . . . in so-called "time-future".

It is not in my memory. I have not been there and witnessed it. How can I be so certain that time-future exists? I can never know time-future. For as soon as the "future" is known, it is present. It is an odd thought . . . but it seems likely that I will not know that I am dead. So why should I fear an event that I will never know . . . nor be able to remember because there will be no historical time left to remember it in?

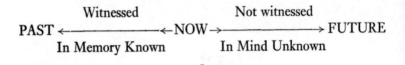

	Witnessed		Not witnessed	
PAST ←		←NOW→		→ FUTURE
	In Memory Known		In Mind Unknown	

*

NOW . . .

I stand on the brink of a precipice.

Behind me stretches the "country that I have crossed" to reach this point; ahead of me lies the unknown . . .

But do I accept and believe that it is unknown?

Do we not all have ideas about the future in the same way that we believe in the past? Do we not hasten to "create" a future in the same way that we "re-create" a past?

Now, as you read this page, do you not presume there will be another one overleaf to read in a future minute?

If you are asked, "What are you going to do tomorrow?", will you not think and, usually, then say, "I am going to do so and so"?

You do not *know* what you will do tomorrow, nor even that there will be a tomorrow, but you may be able to *remember* what is planned for tomorrow!

We have *plans* for the future.

How do we make such plans?

*

As I remember "yesterday"—the events that took place, the things that happened, what "I did"—I notice a pattern emerging. The events took place in a sequence. One event appeared to lead into another in what might be called a "lawful" progression.

For example, taking an ordinary and simple pattern:

I woke from sleep; I opened my eyes; I got up out of bed; I washed; I dressed; perhaps I had breakfast . . . and then I continued the day in the way peculiar to me. (In other words, I followed a basic framework or habitual pattern that has gradually been established as the usual pattern of my life.) There are innumerable ways in which we occupy ourselves or fill the day—we go to

46

school, or we go to work, or we do the housework . . . and so on.

What is important (for our security?) is that we have a planned pattern, a continuous line to pursue, a sequence where one event leads into another. (And the tragedy for the old who have been conditioned by a lifetime of such sequence is that they reach the stage of physical decline when it becomes increasingly impossible to pursue a planned future.)

*

And so, I learn through conditioning to "create" the future of each day, each week, each month, each year . . . and even "my whole future life". And I adopt patterns and sequences which I follow and one event appears to lead into another in continuous succession in lawful order. (I do not, usually!, go to work, then have my breakfast, then get up from bed and then open my eyes and then wake from sleep.)

One event carries me to the next . . . and, believing time to be continuous, I believe that it moves forward, and has a direction.

The sun rises, the darkness dissolves into light, the day begins . . . and will move forward to its end. It is the Law.

This "natural law and order" makes a profound impression on the way I think. It leads me to *expect*. The constant repetition of day and night leads me to *expect* a *continuation* of succeeding day and night.

In this way, the future is not "unknown" to me—in my *expectations*. I can avoid the fact, do not have to admit, that in truth it is *not* known.

I will say, without a moment's hesitation, that in the future from *now* the sun will set and darkness will once more return to the earth where I am, and that that in turn will be followed by another day and another night and another day. When I go to sleep tonight, I will wake up tomorrow. Should a night fall that never ends, or a day dawn that never ends, then one of the great fundamental laws that rules my life from birth to death will have been broken

47

and with it will go all existence, as I witness it . . . and that will include me.

This ordered progress of, or through, passing time is remembered by me now as I visualise the future and imagine the same order stretching ahead of me.

Do I, I begin to wonder, *shape* the future by drawing upon what I remember of the past?

Although my "plans" for the future are often thwarted, interfered with, by "accident", by factors that I cannot predict, do I not persistently continue to try to "create" my future?

The more we look into the phenomenon, the stranger it becomes.

Consider how you "do" something.

Leaving aside the habitual little things that you do automatically without thinking about them (because they no longer have to be visualised), how do you actually motivate yourself into doing something?

Do you not visualise or imagine it first?

And then, having planned it, do you not set out to fulfil it?

For example, you cannot get to a destination without first planning how to get there. Do I not go to "meet" what is already "created" in my mind?

So, am I not continually shaping and creating the future for "me" *before* I actually live it? (Just as, in Genesis, Man was created by God before he came to life.)

And what is your fundamental motive in creating your future?

When we look "behind" all our motivation, our desires, our ambitions . . . are we not looking for that which will provide happiness?

*

Certain things I remember made me happy; other things I remember made me unhappy—or, at least, that is how I tend to think.

But do "things" or "events" *really* have such power? Can they *make* me "happy" or "unhappy"?

What do we mean by these words?

48

To be "happy" could be described as "being in a state of contentment". When we are happy, we do not want, at that moment, things to be different. We are at peace with ourselves and with the world about us.

And when we are unhappy?

We refer back to the past, and remember that there was happiness.

And, in memory, that happiness will be linked with certain places, certain people, certain situations, certain events . . . And so we believe, not unnaturally, that the places, the people, the situations, the events were responsible for our "happiness". And then we further believe that if we want to be happy again, we must experience again similar re-creations of those originals . . .

We are very persistent in this re-creation . . . but, does it *really* work that way?

How is it that a place, a person, a situation, an event can make us happy?

What is this "happiness" that we re-collect?

What causes it?

How does it manifest itself?

What does it do?

*

"Happiness" is a "state of being". We speak of "*being* happy".

It is felt. We speak of "*feeling* happy".

But we cannot predict it, manufacture it, possess it, command it.

It comes upon us, we feel it, we are complete and content; and it goes and we are discomforted, feel incomplete, discontented.

There are no words adequate to describe the feelings—of being happy and being unhappy.

*

Pain is a sensation that to varying degrees invades and disturbs our thinking process. If we are "in pain" the attention of mind is constantly drawn to it. If it is pain in the body, we seek to discover the reason and to alleviate (which means literally "to make light") the pain and remove the cause of it.

This must be a familiar experience for all of us. In the context of this chapter all that it is important to see is that we naturally choose *not to be in pain*. We prefer to be without the pain; we try to restore the balance, the completeness, the wholeness of the body. We seek to reinstate the lawful processes of the physical organism.

And so with mental "pain". The mind's discomforts and discontents are many. The balance—our equanimity—is thrown by all manner of influences. Because we think that our happiness depends on the circumstances surrounding us, and we are always referring back to memories of more auspicious situations, we continually judge what is happening as being conducive or militating against the state of our happiness.

So our "wholeness" is divided as we alternate between pursuit of comfort and pleasure (wherein we think we will find the happiness) and avoidance of pain (wherein we fear we will suffer unhappiness).

But both sets of dualities—the physical and the mental—are based upon our memory of the past and our expectations in the future. It is only because I remember a time when I was not in pain that the desire for the present pain to end as soon as possible in the future occurs to me. If I had never been without pain, how could I know that a painless state could exist?

So, here I am, NOW, always on the brink, always poised between memory and expectation, always trying to maintain balance and contentment. Always the past, coming into the present, creating the pattern for the future. Banished from the paradise of Eden . . . longing for the fulfilment of the "Promised Land".

*

With one eye on the past and one eye on the future, how often do we witness NOW?

We come back to one of the questions with which we began the book, "How long is NOW?"

Or, to put it another way, "Where does the future begin?"

Is there any such thing as "the future"?

If something does not exist before it takes place NOW, does it have any reality? Or do *we* create its reality?

Do we not spend a great part of our waking life dreaming about, thinking about, worrying about . . . the future? Indeed, does not all our conditioning encourage us to do just this? If we do not do this or that now . . . we will not pass our exams, achieve our ambitions, earn enough money, arrive at our destination . . . in the future.

The list of our hopes and fears for the future is manifold but so deep is our conditioning that it is very difficult for us to imagine any other possibility. We must always be preparing now . . . for what is to come.

Why?

Because, if we do not, then when the unknown future comes we will be naked, without any resource with which to meet events . . . or so we tend to believe.

*

We seem to be in a situation like that in the famous fable of the ant and the grasshopper. If we sing all summer long like the grasshopper and do not lay up stores like the busy ant . . . what will befall us when winter comes and food is scarce? Because we have not worked for the future, we will go hungry, we may even starve; it will be painful. And so the fable seems to tell us: Learn from the past and work for the future.

But let us pursue the implications a little further.

The winter has come. The ant has plenty of food; the grasshopper is starving. The future has become the present.

The ant remembers the past summer as a time when it worked busily storing food for now. It likewise imagines that the future to come will be another summer when it will have to work hard again to store food for the winter beyond that.

And what of the poor, starving grasshopper? It remembers the past summer of long, warm days when it hopped from blade to blade and sang to its heart's content. Now, it must surely die— but what a blissful summer it was!

And the ant will live for ever? No; just postponing the inevitable. And the ant's "philosophy"? Keep working; that way it will last as long as possible.

Of course, much could arise out of debating the wisdom of either creature but, in the most simple terms, is it not one of the great dilemmas that confront us all?

Death . . .

Given that it will come . . . so we are conditioned to believe . . . inevitably . . . "in the future" . . . what do we do NOW?

Should we enjoy NOW . . . if we can?

Is it a case of *either* "singing" or "working" . . . NOW?

What *is* life for?

Why *was* I born?

Why *am* I here?

What will be my fate?

*

Of course, in purely practical terms—that is to say, for the well-being, maintenance and survival of the body—it would be unwise not to heed the learning, lessons and experience of the past. And we would become nothing more than idle "vegetables" if we did not plan to ensure provision of what we need.

So, past experience, influencing the present, modifies future plans . . . NOW.

And future plans, "created" in the present, attempt to eliminate past mistakes and failures . . . NOW.

The value of past and future—the possibility of enriching the present—is really here and NOW.

But we tend not to be present, here and NOW. The mind wanders off into the past . . . regretting mistakes, recalling past success and times of happiness. Or it wanders off into the future . . . anxious that plans will not be fulfilled, dreaming of future success and happiness.

Where, then, is the reality?

Is it here and NOW . . . or somewhere in the past or the future?

Is NOW even in the same "plane" or dimension as past and future?

We have asked, "How long is NOW?", "Does it have duration?"

Through observing your own experience, surely NOW cannot belong to passing time at all?

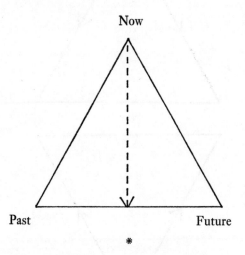

*

Are the past and the future relevant?

"Relevant" is related to "relieve" which means "to lift, to raise up again, to lighten, to make light again".

Can anything be relevant at any time other than NOW?

*

We not only live and contend with our memories of the past; we also live and contend with possibilities for the future. It is never enough that we have survived all that has happened to us on the journey thus far; we are not allowed to stop and rest; there is always further to go and things that are yet to happen to us. And at the end of the journey in which we are never other than nomads—when we continually have to leave where we are—we have no option but to pass over into death.

What comfort is there for us? Is there the promise of anything that we can hope for?

53

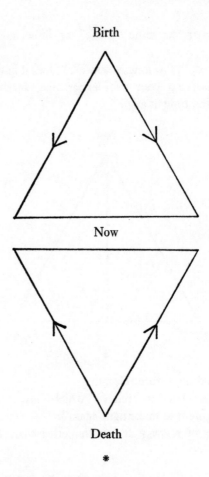

Birth

Now

Death

*

The only comfort, the only hope, must seem to lie in understanding the moment NOW.

That is all we have. It is the only reality.

The past is a vague collection of "two-dimensional" memories.

The future is a vague projection of "two-dimensional" dreams.

NOW is another dimension.

NOW is real, is unified, is timeless, limitless.

NOW is our only relevant experience.

NOW is like a one-dimensional centre, located in any given moment by all the pasts and futures which inform and describe it.

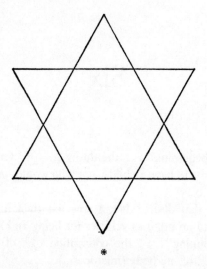

*

To understand this symbol would be liberation—the resolution of all past and future sufferings—to be "within" the Law and yet free of limitation by it.

It is the symbol of Judaism, the Star of David.

Six

"Before the beginning" . . . the desire . . . of "God" to create?
. . . of my parents to have a child? . . . who would, *in time*, become
me?

Did *I* know that desire? No, I was not then in the world. I
had no body and no mind as vehicles for being and knowing.

"In the beginning" . . . the conception . . . of the Universe
(macrocosm) . . . of my body (microcosm).

Did I know that conception? Was *I* there, at the conception of
me? The potential for a body was created as the duality of paternal
sperm and maternal ovum fused in union; and from that moment
the vehicle that was to become my body began to form in the
world's time. But *I* do not remember being there. Had the mind
that was to become my mind begun?

"In the beginning" . . . the continuous forming, in the "darkness"
of the womb . . . the "days" of gestation as the body miraculously
"knew the law" of forming itself in preparation for birth. And
somewhere in that "timeless" dark, a division took place as the
body "chose" to become male or female. It could not be said that
I chose which to become, could it?

At that crucial point, unity was lost. There was the first becoming
one part *as opposed to* another part. The fundamental duality
(halving) that would condition "the life to come" was introduced
at a time that *I* do not remember. Already, some law was laying
down the foundations of my fate. And *I* did not know. For had what
I call "my mind" even yet begun? Had *I* yet begun?

"In the beginning" . . . the birth . . . the instantaneous appearance of the Universe? . . . the appearance from darkness into
light so that the darkness was known to be divided from the light

. . . the becoming manifest of a body which was to be the vehicle for my being . . . taking its place as a separate entity in the history of the world. One breath and it was independently alive . . . complete, and yet, being *either* male *or* female, incomplete. Is this the moment that my mind began? Do *I* remember yet? Had *I* yet begun?

"In the beginning" . . . childhood . . . body still growing towards maturity, mind now receiving impressions from the world and forming patterns of behaviour in response. The mind that is to be called "my mind" begins to accumulate a content of learning within the time and law of the physical world. Yet do *I* remember? Have *I* yet begun?

*

The body grows to the limits imposed by natural law. *I* cannot dictate the limits of that form.

At first, "things" happen to the body and there is simply reaction. *I* do not dictate what that reaction will be nor what happens. For am *I* there?

But then, as past experience is impressed in memory, so comes the ability of the mind to desire repetition of pleasure and to fear repetition of pain. So "self-generated planning" begins and deliberate choices for actions are taken. Is this where *I* begin . . . with the first act of my own will? Perhaps . . . but, if so, then I must have been "asleep" to it if I do not remember it?

The time of "innocence" passes with my ability to make a wilful action. ("Innocence" means literally "not hurting" and the ability to hurt is something of which I am now capable.) So the mind is introduced to "social" law (possibly both secular and religious) and limits are imposed on what I may or may not do and say.

But am *I* yet born? Was *I* there to remember what happened? Perhaps . . . and, if so, did *I* then begin with the first thing remembered?

Why, after all the weeks and months, possibly years, of the forming of the body and mind is something suddenly experienced which can be remembered in such a way that it can be recalled as

c 57

a memory? What is it that enables the first "memorable" memory
... and then through passing time succeeding re-call-able memories?

Is there sudden heightened awareness of a particular moment?
Is something memorable because it stimulates or shocks the mind
so that attention is focused strongly on it? Is it to do with what we
learn to call "consciousness"?

*

What is "consciousness"?

What is this "light of consciousness" which illuminates our
present experience?

At what point, in the evolution which we have so far described
in this chapter, can there be said to be "consciousness"?

Is the beginning of "*I*" something to do with consciousness?

We would ordinarily say that as soon as the first breath is taken
the new-born baby is "conscious".

What happened at the first moment of consciousness?

Did "spirit" (whatever that may mean!) enter the body . . . and
perhaps cause the conception of mind . . . at the moment the body
breathed its first "breath of life"?

What is that "spirit" which imbues the mind with consciousness?

Herein lies an awe-inspiring mystery!

Just *what* is this consciousness which we take utterly for granted?

So absorbed in the contrived importance of the total fiction
(because created and superimposed by ourselves) of our ephemeral
concerns about daily life do we become that we utterly ignore the
miracle of genesis . . . the coming into existence of this miraculous
body-vehicle, the mystery of "mind", the incomprehensible
phenomenon of "consciousness" . . . and so on.

*

Let us, however, pursue a little further, as best we can!

The experience of genesis . . . the ever-present "in the beginning"
. . . continues.

At some point in "normal" development a crucial event takes
place which, we assume, is particular to the human being amongst

all creatures. There comes a moment, which we may well not even remember now, when another "birth" takes place—the moment when *I* become "aware of myself" as an individual entity.

Put rather simplistically,there must have been a first time when I said to myself, "I am . . . I am here . . . in this world". I become aware of "me". In other words, we could say that consciousness arose, by virtue of and "through" the body, of being here as a particular person.

Is that when *I* began? . . . when *I* was first conscious of being *me*? Do I remember that moment or not?

The mystery deepens.

Can I remember suddenly realising "I am"?

Can I remember "I am" . . . *in the past*?

*

Why can I remember certain incidents, scenes, feelings?

Was it because of the strength of the power of consciousness at the time?

What law governs "spirit" or consciousness?

Is it "above" law?

Perhaps an event is remembered if it is particularly stimulating, especially emotionally . . . if it "wakes me up"?

Perhaps something is only remembered if I witness it *consciously*!

Perhaps *I* am/is "consciousness"?

*

What wakes me up to "being here now", fully conscious?

What causes me to remember "I am . . . NOW . . . here"?

What "enters" to re-mind me of my present existence?

And when it happens . . . it is as if it is a new birth, a genesis. Suddenly . . . I am here and know it.

*

I is here, NOW.

I cannot be, in the past. *I* never has been . . . in the past. *I* never will *be*, in the future. *I* cannot *be*, in the future.

I am, NOW . . . or not at all.

I appear . . . and disappear . . . from moment to moment.

I did not "begin" in the past . . . any more than *I* will "end" in the future.

I—consciousness of "is-ness"—is *always*, for ever, present NOW.

*

But we are jumping ahead—to the simultaneous exodus.

What else happened in my evolution?

From the moment I first became able to initiate self-willed action to "better" the future or to avoid a "worse" future, and from the moment I first became aware of myself (the "forming of Eve" out of identification of myself as the body), I began to contrive my *continuation*. The wishing to ensure my continuation could be described as the "female" quality at work—this quality being concerned with re-creation, sustenance, maintenance, security, conservation, preservation, protection, survival of the species . . . and so on. (As opposed to the "male" quality and characteristic in me, seen as idealistic, creative, destructive).

This instinctive "female" motivation—to survive, to continue, to create a settled and secure place and position—moulds my personality. It is built on the foundation of my physical existence; my body being the foundation of my life and living. And I perceive continuity of existence as a challenge and struggle to work and acquire what I need and want, and a countering of that which militates against me.

*

And unto Adam he said, Because thou hast harkened unto the voice of thy wife, and hast eaten of the tree, of which I commanded thee, saying, Thou shalt not eat of it: cursed is the ground for thy sake; in sorrow shalt thou eat of it all the days of thy life;

Thorns also and thistles shall it bring forth to thee; and thou shalt eat the herb of the field;

In the sweat of thy face shalt thou eat bread, till thou return unto

60

the ground; for out of it wast thou taken: for dust thou art, and unto dust shalt thou return.

And Adam called his wife's name Eve; because she was the mother of all living.

Unto Adam also and to his wife did the Lord God make coats of skins, and clothed them.

(Genesis, 3: 17–21)

*

And increasingly, as my "protective clothing" of personality forms, I become independent of my parents. The more I build myself as an individual—inevitably and naturally—the less am I simply the product of my father and mother.

*

And Adam said, This is now bone of my bones, and flesh of my flesh: she shall be called Woman, because she was taken out of Man.

Therefore shall a man leave his father and his mother, and shall cleave unto his wife: and they shall be one flesh.

(Genesis, 2: 23–24)

*

But, the more identified I become with my body, the more I become aware of duality and incompleteness.

I become aware of other body-identified persons as being different . . . of the "other" sex.

There is "born" in my body a new and individual will, or "ego-power".

Sex energy arises within me . . . and I become aware of the desire to resolve the duality, to satisfy the incompleteness, to heal the separation, to unify the division . . . and I look for the complementary other "half" in the world.

The will to search, hunt and compete surges up within me . . . the "male" in me whether my body be male or female in form.

It surges up, when I reach puberty, in a manner that is irrepressible. Coping with it permeates my whole life.

61

I step into a new "chapter" in my genesis. The power of pro-creation initiates my adulthood. I enter into the realm of generation and its laws . . . of cause and effect, *ad infinitum*.

*

And Adam knew Eve his wife; and she conceived, and bare Cain, and said, I have gotten a man from the Lord.

(Genesis, 4: 1)

*

But . . . seemingly coincidentally, another "initiation" is taking place.

With the maturing of the body comes a new "phase" of mind.

My thinking, which has been concerned with manipulation of the "things" of this world, makes a quantum jump into a new dimension. Suddenly (though we are unlikely to remember the "sudden-ness" of that first thought) I am able to think "in abstract".

There is "born" in mind a totally new and different ability . . . to consider my existence, and the existence of all things, and their properties, qualities and laws, "objectively". That is to say, suddenly I am able to witness "in abstract" . . . as if I am apart from all existing phenomena.

This evolving out of my mind of a "subject" which can witness, theorise about, consider, evaluate and judge all "objects" creates, as it were, a "space" in mind in which extraordinary questions may form.

Who am I?

Why was I born?

Why am I here?

What happens when I die?

And so on . . .

Is this when *I* begin?

At the same time as the "female" in me looks to the world for fulfilment, continuity, completion, perfection . . . so the "male" in me . . . the "I" . . . "arises", "enters", or however the experience

62

may be described. The "spirit" is experienced? The spiritual life begins?

I am again divided . . . between "heaven" and "earth".

*

Such questions may move me deeply.

And I try to cope with them as best as I am able.

But do I find really satisfying answers?

Do I have the strength, the power, the experience, the ability, the knowledge, to answer them?

Usually, they seem quite beyond me and soon, in any case, there is little or no time to give attention to them.

There is so much going on in my life that is new to me and the world demands so much that I am dominated by the challenge to search for my place and fulfilment in it. The questions tend to die down and become forgotten in my preoccupation with living "my life".

*

And she (Eve) again bare his brother Abel. And Abel was a keeper of sheep, but Cain was a tiller of the ground.

And in process of time it came to pass, that Cain brought of the fruit of the ground an offering unto the Lord.

And Abel, he also brought of the firstlings of his flock and of the fat thereof. And the Lord had respect unto Abel and to his offering:

But unto Cain and to his offering he had not respect. And Cain was very wroth, and his countenance fell.

And the Lord said unto Cain, Why art thou wroth? and why is thy countenance fallen?

If thou doest well, shalt thou not be accepted? and if thou doest not well, sin lieth at the door. And unto thee shall be his desire, and thou shalt rule over him.

And Cain talked with Abel his brother: and it came to pass, when they were in the field, that Cain rose up against Abel his brother, and slew him.

. . .

63

And Adam knew his wife again; and she bare a son, and called his name Seth: For God, said she, hath appointed me another seed instead of Abel, whom Cain slew.

And to Seth, to him also there was born a son; and he called his name Enos: then began men to call upon the name of the Lord.

(Genesis, 4: 2–8, 25, 26)

*

The "spiritual" questions may lead a person to try to discover the meaning of life; and such a search will inevitably involve enquiry into the nature of religion.

Indeed, we could go further and say that out of such questions arose the concept of "religion" in the first place.

Because our memory is limited by the necessity for the mind-vehicle being present to contain that memory, we cannot remember before we were born. Because there is no memory of *before birth*, there can only be but vague imaginings of *after death* if we are, as it were, trapped within the confines of the body's passing time.

So, in our predicament, such questions as "Where did I come from?" and "Where am I going to?" challenge us to search for the "way out" (the exodus).

All the faith religions that man has adopted during the history of his presence here on earth have attempted answers to such questions. How adequate the explanations prove to be must depend on the individual, for there is no universally accepted, absolutely proven teaching in the history of world religion. (If there were, there would be no more problems!) So the efficacy of the religion depends upon individual comprehension, upon the degree of understanding of the chosen form of religion, upon the accuracy of the individual's witnessing of events and his experience of them, and upon the degree of his ability to have faith, believe in, his particular concept of "god".

The mental image or concept of "god" cannot be conveyed as an experience from one person to another. "God" cannot be held up for you to look at; "god" cannot be discussed as an object; "god" cannot be intellectually "proved"; because "god" does not exist as an image in memory; "images" belong to the "created" world only.

To try to conceive of "god" is similar to trying to comprehend the concept of limitless space, of eternity, of infinity or of no-thing. The ordinary workings of mind do not have the capacity to transcend their own limitations bound as they are to the law and form of that which is already created. If "god" had any property, form, image, quality, it could be described; so then we have to ask, "Who created that property, form, image, quality, or whatever?"

In fact even to give a name such as "god" to that all-transcending concept is to ascribe simply a man-invented name to an idea. It is not "what it is itself". Which is why the Jewish faith forbids the speaking of "the name of God"; perhaps not so much because it is ignorant to think one may do so because, in fact, it is *not possible*. Any presumption as to being able to do so is "taking the name in vain".

Is there any hope at all then that Man—both individually and as a species—can ever realise the nature of his being, the reason for his existence and the purpose of his presence here on earth? If we will never know where we came from nor where we are going to, what is the point of being here? Is any worldly explanation sufficient—that of the evolutionist, the biologist, the physicist, the astronomer, the philosopher, the ecologist, the sociologist . . . if they have one?

And is the theologian's answer any more meaningful than anyone else's?

*

The ancient scriptures of the Torah begin, as we have been saying, with the stories of creation. If taken literally, it seems that all the work of creation was completed in six days—and the seventh day was a day of rest. (What did God do after that—apart from speaking to certain people from time to time?)

The story certainly pre-supposes the "god" who brought it all about. It does not explain *why* he did it nor *how* he did it, nor even *who* he is. To what in me therefore does it hope to relate? What am I expected to make of it?

The moment I begin to attempt to make sense of the story in the terms of my conditioned learning of the world, I fail miserably.

And to the extent that I may require that stories should be logical, and that I expect someone of the stature of "god" to be reasonable, I may even become frustrated enough to protest! The plot reads as though God deliberately set a trap for Adam and Eve. If "he" really had not wanted them to eat certain fruit, "he" could easily have prevented it. But then to get angry with Adam and punish him so severely! And why should we suffer for what Adam did? If the Lord God created everything he must have created the evil as well as the good. Why set up the temptation to sin in the first place? And so on . . .

So, what are we implying and suggesting by what we have written so far?

We have said that in embarking on consideration of the Judaic scriptures (and the Pentateuch in particular) we are not, in this age of scientific conditioning, going to find much satisfaction in them if we take them simply in literal terms.

But, even allowing for the fact that we are using English translation from the Hebrew (and some would say an inaccurate translation at that, especially as it has been transferred through several languages in between), there may perhaps be an extraordinary message contained in those stories if we consider them as allegories of *our own experience* of life.

The validity for doing this can *only* lie in the response of the individual—you!

If such an exploration actually illuminates your past experience —your genesis—and you recognise and feel the parallel, then will you not say, "Ah! I see! . . . At last I am beginning to understand what happened!"

From what we have hinted at so far (and it should be borne in mind that it is only the view of the authors of this book), it really does seem that the Judaic scriptures reveal the Law . . . as it defines the limits of experience of each and every human being in this creation.

This is an awesome, unique and extraordinary revelation.

It requires the mind to use all its powers and capacities to their utmost . . . to trace the "plot", as it were, and to decipher it in relation to experience. We must be able to observe, analyse, feel and compare every nuance of that experience . . . from the point at which we are, NOW.

The difficulty is that it challenges head-on the body-identified and generated view of chronological time . . . of past and future. And it challenges all my assumptions about myself, and who and what I think I am. And it demands that we recognise what laws operate in the "realms" of body, mind and "spirit". And we may find that what the Law reveals—perhaps paradoxically—is the nature of Freedom.

*

So far we have touched on Genesis which describes processes of birth—physical, mental and spiritual—"in" time and "out" of it; processes which bring us, phase by phase, into existence, leading us into involvement at different levels of creation. It ranges through such concepts as desire, conception, birth, duality, past, future, present, memory, expectation, identity, parents, offspring . . . and so on. And it suggests that what takes place in these beginnings is natural and lawful.

What option do we have but to accept the fact of our existence?

After the various "births", "beginnings" and "emergences" that we have mentioned—and we have only touched briefly on a few verses of the first chapters of the first book of the Bible—we may follow and draw upon all manner of concept before we reach the final passages of Deuteronomy, the fifth book of the Pentateuch. And they will surely also be found to exercise our minds as we seek to understand our maturing experience of the world—of its trials and tribulations, of its joys and sorrows—until the body dies.

And after that?

Or should we really ask such a question?

Is what we are really searching for in the future?
The moment that I die, when it comes, will be NOW.
What might I expect to understand in that moment?
For as surely as all beginnings are NOW, so are all endings NOW.

*

*And the Lord said unto him, This is the land which I sware unto
Abraham, unto Isaac, and unto Jacob, saying, I will give it unto thy
seed: I have caused thee to see it with thine eyes, but thou shalt not
go over thither.*
*So Moses the servant of the Lord died there in the land of Moab,
according to the word of the Lord.*

(Deuteronomy, 34: 4, 5)

*

The Jewish people consider themselves as the descendents of
Adam and Eve and of their offspring, known as the children or
tribes of Israel.

The Torah—which is a Hebrew word meaning "doctrine" or
"teaching"—traces the story of the children of Israel through
their wanderings and their captivities, their victories and their
defeats, their times of plenty and their times of suffering. It is a
journey that begins after banishment from the Garden of Eden
until their arrival at the threshold of the Promised Land.

EASTWARD IN EDEN — WANDERINGS OF THE TRIBES — PROMISED LAND
BIRTH — EXPERIENCE THROUGH LIFE — DEATH

In other words, the sacred *teaching* of the Jewish religion is
also the sacred *history* (memory) of their tribe.

Relying upon memory, and the continual repetition of that
memory, they have wrought over thousands of years since their
nomadic desert beginnings, a code of behaviour—both social and
religious—based upon *experience in life*. (Indeed, many of their
most treasured ceremonies are precisely memory-aids, symbols
to remind them of past events).

The Judaic tradition expressed in the Torah and the Hindu

68

teachings expressed in the Vedas are two of the most ancient religious expositions at present known (and neither of them are based on the teachings of an individual man). And they still remain, vital and sacred after several millennia.

Judaism reaches back to the beginnings of civilisation when men first began to live together and to require a social code and law. And that law has been observed and maintained, unchanged in principle, until this present day, despite the scattering of the tribe to all parts of the world and despite all the sophisticated, scientific and technological developments over the centuries.

The discipline of the Judaic faith and the strength that it imparts gives the religion a remarkable presence in the world—one that is quite disproportionate to the number of its adherents (compared with say Christians, Moslems, Hindus or Buddhists).

Why should it persist so strongly?

Because maybe an emotional instinct prevails over intellectual logic?

Because maybe the instinct to preserve tribal identity prevails over mass integration?

Whatever the reason, an extraordinary, powerful element of conviction and exclusivity has always stood at the heart of Jewish belief.

The most common of Hebrew prayers, recited three or four times a day by the orthodox Jew, begins with the words, *Shma Yisrael*; it should be the last prayer that he utters on his deathbed.

Hear, O Israel: The Lord our God, the Lord is One!—And thou shalt love the Lord thy God, with all thy heart, and with all thy soul, and with all thy might. And these words, which I command thee this day, shall be upon thy heart, and thou shalt teach them diligently to thy children, and thou shalt talk of them when thou sittest in thy house, and when thou walkest by the way, and when thou liest down, and when thou risest up. And thou shalt bind them for a sign upon thy hand, and they shall be for frontlets between thine eyes. And thou shalt write them upon the door-posts of thy house and upon thy gates.

Seven

So we have become what we are—NOW.

Do you think you had any option but to be what you are—NOW?

From the moment of your parents' desire, through conception, gestation, birth, babyhood, childhood, into adolescence and adulthood, has not your fate been "sealed"? Has not the Law been laid down for you?

I am what I am—NOW.

How could I possibly be other than I am—NOW?

Can I ever become other than what I am going to be?

If there is to be any change, can I possibly change the "future"?

How can I change what is not here and NOW?

So, I may say, "If I change NOW, the future will be changed"; but, again, how can what is not yet be made different?

So, what possibility is there?

Only NOW . . . and only to discover that which is "above" or "beyond" the Law?

*

And so we are born. We become, come-to-be. And our genesis is in memory. Our fate is written.

We emerge from the womb, incarnated, formed, sexed, a manifest image of the species Man, of Adam.

The cord is cut that joins us to the mother ("earth")—the cord through which we have "breathed" and been sustained, through which life-blood has pumped into us and out of us, through which we have been enlivened. The cord is cut and for an instant we are poised between existence and non-existence. We breathe in and we are independently alive . . . poised between "earth" and "heaven", between "time" and "eternity", between the finite and the infinite. And we breathe out.

And at that moment we come under Law.

At that moment we are committed to *life* . . . and we are destined to *die*.

*

And the Lord God said, Behold, the man is become as one of us, to know good and evil: and now, lest he put forth his hand, and take also of the tree of life, and eat, and live for ever:

Therefore the Lord God sent him forth from the garden of Eden, to till the ground from whence he was taken.

*

We become involved in the earthly life and it becomes an obsession with us. And the obsession is based upon a natural assumption.

Thus our beginning or becoming is assumed to be a *result*—— in a chain of results stretching back into "a distant past" before man existed.

But though I may be the result of my parents' copulation in past time, what *causes* my being here *now*?

*

The assumed chain of events which provides a series of results is one thing; but the cause of the whole process is quite another.

Causes, we soon realise, are far more elusive than explicable results. No sooner do we try to trace back from one result to that which caused it, than we find that that cause was itself the result of something else.

And the cause is ever-elusive because it lies "above" or "beyond" the conditioned learning of the mind vehicle which can only trace movement in time. The ordinary mind can only hold, remember and "juggle with" results. What we call mind is, in itself, a result.

So, once we start searching for the cause of things, we enter a realm for which the mind has no data and which it is not capable of remembering.

And yet "looking for the cause" has always intrigued the mind of man. Although much occupied with physical survival and pleasure on earth (his "mother") he has persistently searched for the identity of that which caused his creation (his "father"). For centuries past the search was primarily through philosophy and religion (hence the emergence of such concepts and names as "Creator", "God", "Jehovah", "Father Almighty" and so on). Today however the focus of the search is primarily through science and is couched in scientific terms—whether it be through looking "inwards" to the microscopic realms of the micro-biologist or "outwards" to the space realms of the astro-physicist.

And simultaneously, on the scale of his body, he also searches for the causes of his own destruction. The psychiatrists—arguably the "priests" of many societies today—seek the causes of mental illness; and the doctors—while generally seeking to remove or cure the symptoms or results of disease or sickness—hope to discover what caused the malady in the first place, and thus reveal the "elixir of life".

With results that we deem undesirable, we assume that all would be well if we could eliminate the causes of those effects; we tend not to accept that the results are lawful; we tend to think of them as accidental afflictions. We tend to think that the cause of our suffering is "out there" and that we are simply victims of misfortune.

*

But supposing a bio-chemist did manage to "create" life; what do you imagine he would then want to do? What results do you suppose he would then set about causing?

And supposing he managed to find the key to "eternal life", or found the means to avoid death indefinitely, what do you imagine would happen on earth?

And if the geneticist managed to find a way to manipulate human genes to a desired effect, do you think he would attempt to "create" a perfect man? What would be his image of such a man—or woman?

In other words, what do you suppose would happen if man, having "eaten of the tree of knowledge of good and evil", succeeded also in "taking of the tree of life . . . and lived for ever"?

*

Let us look a little further at "cause" . . . because . . . be-cause . . . the causing to be; and at "effect" . . . the "out of that which is made or done"; and at "result" . . . "jump back".

The Law states that the Universe is One. Why? *Because* by its own definition the Universe is everything. There cannot be two or three universes *because* combined together, added together, they would immediately "jump back" to being one total Universe.

Likewise "you" are by Law unique. There cannot be two or three "yous". It is impossible for you to meet another you *because* you cannot be in two places at once since you only have one physical body.

*

The most lawful science or knowledge recognised by man is that of mathematics—numbers and their relationships. The four processes—addition, subtraction, multiplication and division—quantify all "events" in physical existence. Location in space and measurement of time can be described with number. The whole process of our life on earth can be described in terms of location, space, time, movement, increase, decrease.

At the purely physical level, this may seem frighteningly predictable and mechanical. Simply in terms of counting, numbers seem only lifeless and calculating, even if we allow that their functional ability to quantify is very useful in the daily business of life—not only in numbers of units but for defining area, volume and so on.

But in restricting them to this purely practical function, they are effectively deprived of their remarkable power.

*

How often we use them . . . simply as an inexhaustible supply of units!

And how little we contemplate what they can tell us . . . if we pause to consider the laws they embody and their properties.

We cannot go into this in depth in this book but let us consider a little . . .

We use only ten hieroglyphs—the digits which in Arabic look something like this: 0, 1, 2, 3, 4, 5, 6, 7, 8, 9. All other numbers are based on just these ten.

Why ten?

Because every possible pattern and relationship of which the human mind can conceive can be described by just that number —no more, no less?

Were they invented arbitrarily?

Or did experience show that that number were needed?

Try inventing another and fitting it in!

You would have to devise a completely different system of counting!

The question is whether you would be able to demonstrate that more or less different hieroglyphs are needed.

*

Let us have a look at one of the hieroglyphs—1 (called "the first". Although we have written "0" before it in the section above, "0" can "go anywhere". It does not have a defined relationship with any of the others, since it does not belong to the "finite" world).

The beginning of our introduction to mathematics is usually addition:

$$1 + 1 = 2$$
$$1 + 2 = 3$$
$$1 + 3 = 4$$

But where did the first "1" come from?

Once I have One I can imagine another One and add it to the first One and call it Two . . . and so on. But, again, where did the first One appear from?

Then I may start to learn subtraction:

$$4 - 1 = 3$$
$$3 - 1 = 2$$
$$2 - 1 = 1$$
$$1 - 1 = 0$$

Zero!

What is that?

Nothing?

If I have One and I take it away from itself, I have Nothing!

How can One be taken away from itself? And if that equals Nothing, where has the One gone to?

*

"But," someone may say, "it means one 'something' . . . a pencil, or a house, or a cow . . ."

But, quite apart from the fact that this is again reducing number to mere quantities, how can you take One cow away from itself? And if you have Two cows and you take One cow away, and say that you only have One cow left, has the other cow disappeared into thin air?

What is it that we were introduced to when we started to learn mathematics?

It begins to seem as though we were introduced to absurdity!

*

And multiplication and division do not seem to help.

$$1 \times 1 = 1$$
$$1 \times 2 = 2$$
$$1 \times 3 = 3$$

What is happening to the first One? Why does it keep disappearing?

Likewise with division:

$$1 \div 1 = 1$$
$$2 \div 1 = 2$$
$$3 \div 1 = 3$$

How can One divided by itself remain itself?

*

And if we try to introduce "o", the situation gets even worse!

Zero can do *nothing* to One if it tries to add itself or subtract itself to or from One, or even if it tries to divide it. But if it multiplies One, the One disappears into Nothing!

So, we might ask, if we can make the One disappear, where has it gone . . . and again, where did it come from in the first place?

*

It is no good saying it comes from the other numbers because all the other numbers are derived from One.

Although even that is not as straightforward as it may seem.

If One does exist . . . then it must be alone . . . *because*, by the law of its definition, if there were another One, then it would not be One!

Therefore, Two, conceived of as two Ones, is impossible . . . or an illusion.

Therefore, the only possible and valid concept of Two must be as *Two Halves* of *One*.

This means that the only possible multiplication is by division! (And "division" means "seeing two or double").

*

Do we then begin to feel and comprehend the power of the Law of numbers?

"Before the beginning" . . . zero . . . Nothing.

"In the beginning" . . . the appearance of One.

"After the beginning" . . . generation by division . . . Two.

*

Between No-thing, o . . . "limitless space" . . .
and Something, 1 . . . the manifest Universe . . .
is the Great Cause of All . . .
beyond comprehension, beyond proof.
Results can be accounted:
4 dots . . . . plus 4 dots . . . . equal 8 dots . . . .
But where did the concept of the first dot come from?

After the idea "dot" comes the first manifest "dot" and, thereafter, by reproduction, "dots" *ad infinitum*.

*

The One is divided (by having "the female half taken out of itself") and gives rise to Two—and hence all duality from there onwards. The union of the One and Two (addition—ad-do, Latin, "give to"), "male" and "female", produces Three (the "son") and within and from that trinity of inter-action arises all possibilities.

There are fundamentally two "lines of descent" generated from the One which becomes Two—the "male" or Adam line ("odd" numbers, the word "odd" being derived from Old Norse and meaning "third" and connected with "point, angle, triangle") and the "female" or Eve line ("even" numbers). And the first Three, in "triangular" relationship, has three fundamental aspects (for example, the three conditions of force—active, passive and conditioning or neutralising—the characteristics represented by the archetypal Cain, Abel and Seth) running both male and female lines of descent . . . and giving, crucially, the possibility of "ascent".

And the combination of two of the fundamental "trinities", the active and the passive, the male and the female, gives rise to six—in Latin, "*sex*".

And so we might go on . . . to comprehend the laws which govern all relationships and possibilities through the intelligence and characteristics of the nine primal digits and their interaction.

Apart from the fact that this can be a stimulating and revealing study of numbers, and that it is unquestionably crucial to understanding the laws which govern creation (including all man's activities—secular, cultural and religious), why should we introduce it into a book on Judaism?

Partly because, in Hebrew, numbers are represented by letters (or *vice versa*) and therefore the same glyph represents both *sound and law*.

The ramifications of this are enormous and it is crucial to a deeper understanding of the Judaic tradition and its strength.

The Spoken Word (The Teaching) is the Law of the Universe and Man.

*

Hear, O Israel: the Lord our God, the Lord is One!

*

Once this relationship between letter and number is appreciated, so much in the Pentateuch which seems arbitrary, contradictory and meaningless is illuminated. It "explains" all manner of enigma —the number of generations, the meaning of the names of the archetypes, the number of years people lived, the changing of names (God to Lord God, Abram to Abraham, Sarai to Sarah, Jacob to Israel, and so on); even the numbers of the chapters and verses are significant.

*

We cannot exhaustively pursue such a study here in this book but let us remain for a moment with a strange quirk of the English language.

"I", the glyph for the "first person" singular, the subject, is the same as that used for 1, the first number. (We even sometimes use the word "one" when referring to "ourself" . . . particularly to ourselves *objectively*).

We have asked, "Where does 1 (one) come from?"

And we have asked, "Where do I come from?"

*

What can we say about the glyph, its sound, its character, what it represents? What do we instinctively feel and know about it?

It is a male or phallic symbol.

It is alone, al-one, all one.

It is complete and whole.

It is impotent . . . but all possibilities lie within it.

Whilst it is single, it cannot, for example, witness or know itself.

78

The only possibility of any development from this static potential is through itself . . . by dividing itself.

And then . . . conjecture.

But what would be familiar to us in our own experience?

Supposing that the prime, emergent idea or desire were for the One to witness and know itself?

Would it not first have to separate from itself the means whereby it could produce its own likeness and image?

And, having done that, might there not be unforseen repercussions and consequences ("that which comes after or follows as a result; effect; the relation of an effect to its cause . . .")

The "father", having impregnated the "mother" and produced the "son" in his own image, creation is set in motion and new relationships develop.

There will be, independent of the "father", relationship between "mother" and "son".

And a relationship between "father" and "son", independent of the "mother".

And supposing . . . the "son" obtains "will" of its own and forgets the "father", and thinks itself to be the One?

(Supposing the "mother" (like Rebekah) persuades the "son" (like Jacob) to deceive the "father" (Isaac) and steal the "birthright"—as in Genesis, chapter 27).

*

And so the laws multiply, once One has divided itself.

The "wholeness" is lost (unless it be as a perfect "family" triad of "father", "mother" and "son").

And can it ever be retrieved?

Only by *subtraction* of all that is not One.

Only by destruction and dissolution of multiplicity and finally duality, can unity be regained.

Only by surrendering all that one has taken and added to oneself . . . even "life" itself.

*

Thus, not only am I given the power to create but also to destroy.

Or, to be more accurate, my body can be the vehicle for creation or destruction. It can be the instrument both to give life and to take life.

And I think that it is I who have this power; I take upon myself the role of a "god".

But . . . can any father or mother honestly say that he or she created a living child?

If the desire to copulate arises in me, it is "good" (within accepted social circumstances) to take part in creating new life.

But if the desire to destroy or kill arises in me, it is "bad" (unless condoned by society) to be instrumental in taking life.

Why?

Can "I" *actually* take life . . . actually destroy it . . . any more than "I" have the power to give it?

Eight

We have called this book *The Judaic Law*.

The reasons for having done so should be apparent by now—for it seems to us, the authors, that to relate the historical and current performance of Judiasm does not help us very much to understand its inner religious strengths and why the Jewish scriptures inevitably apply to each one of us whether or not we be Jewish by birth.

In other words we are suggesting that the Law written in the Torah—especially in the first book—*is* the Law for you and me . . . whether we recognise and accept it or not . . . whether we label ourselves Jewish, Christian, Muslim, Buddhist, Hindu, atheist, Communist or whatever. There is nothing exclusive about it (on the contrary, it embraces all men) and the "chosen people" has got nothing to do with the "accident" of a particular racial inheritance. The "chosen people" are those who hear and heed the Law. Given birth into existence, that Law *cannot* be avoided; it operates through the very nature of existence. It is simply a question as to whether we are aware of it or not; and, if we are, then there is the possibility of understanding the nature of freedom.

The "father" of all mankind is one and the same (whether it be written, for example, in the form Abram/Abraham or Brahman/Brahma).

One of the most ancient dispensations, describing in Hebrew the laws of genesis and generation, is translated into English at the beginning of what is called the biblical Old Testament.

*

"Testament" may be seen to derive etymologically from the Latin words *testis* meaning "witness" (also the root of "testicle", the

81

essentially male power and function which, in turn, can be related to the phallic "I"—thus endorsing the nature of the "I" as being not only the "witness" but also as being "male" will) and "-ment", a suffix which begs association with *mens-mentis* meaning "mind" rather than the alternative *mentum* which means "chin". It also seems appropriate not to ignore "testa-" as possibly being linked with the feminine noun *testa* which has the meaning "shell or covering".

Thus a number of ideas arise as to the meaning of testament. It suggests in the "male" sense "witness"; and in the "female" sense "shell or covering" which expresses both a sense of protection whilst still immature and also a restrictive limitation which can be broken out of or uncovered (dis-covered).

We have digressed in this exploration but even in this speculation we may find a hint of the purpose of religious scripture. We see the implication of the witness, the "I" standing "outside" or "beyond" the stated Law, and in the female aspect the implication of the Law being a protection and a delineation of the limits within which we are confined as existing beings on earth.

Arising out of only one word is a wealth of explanation.

*

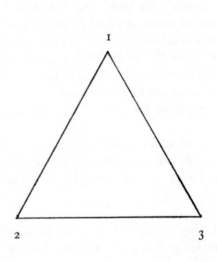

So, to continue . . .

Given the genesis or emergence of the One and its *self-division* into Two, we find as a product of their re-union, Three—the primordial trinity, the three-fold One, which is the cornerstone of so many of the world's religious expositions.

But, in any interaction of duality, there are two possibilities. Either pole or partner may be either active or passive, giving rise to two distinct products or offspring, which may be of different natures.

In the case of the firstborn, Cain, it was Adam (representing the Lord) who was active; "I have gotten a man from the Lord". (Comparable with the divine conception of Jesus through Mary). Whereas for Abel it was simply a case of, "And she again bare his brother . . ." In relation to the world, Cain became active ("a tiller of the ground") and Abel passive ("a keeper of sheep"). Cain is Three (of the odd or "male" line) and Abel Four (of the eve-n or "female" line).

And then?

Is the descent to continue through the "male" Three or the "female" Four? If generation is through simple (and "mechanical") division of the latter, will there be no "male" lineage? Evidently this was not destined to be the Law for Man. Three prevails over Four and begets its own generation (albeit a limited one).

Cain goes to the "land of Nod, on the east of Eden" and "knows" his wife. (Where, one might ask, does she come from?) He begets five generations starting with his son, Enoch, and ending with Lamech, who marries *two wives* to produce the sixth generation—three sons and one daughter (the first recorded "natural" birth of a "female").

Adam then "knew his wife again" and Five, as direct "male" descent from One, is born. ("For God, said she, hath appointed me another seed . . .") This "son", Seth, has nine generations.

The fifth generation of Seth is Enoch (of whom it is said, "And Enoch walked with God: he *was* not; for God took him." He is not said to have "died") and the seventh, Lamech. The eighth generation, Noah, has three sons ("reflecting" Adam and his three sons).

And then?

The "male" line of Cain (Three) is eliminated, by the "flood" (unless Enoch, the first generation of Cain and the fifth of Seth, and Lamech, the fifth of Cain and the seventh of Seth, are related or connected, perhaps being the "same"?)

After the flood, Noah becomes the "new father" of mankind (the new One) which is divided into three lines of descent after "every living substance was destroyed" (as if after Nine all numbers are wiped out and One must begin again as Ten).

*

We cannot pause too often to pursue the above and its implications. It is for those who think they would find value in doing so to interpret for themselves. For the value must ideally lie in investigating and testing for yourself against *your own experience*. If someone else just tells you, you will not necessarily *feel* and *realise* the significance for yourself.

The strength and security of the great scriptures lies in their making the individual work for himself. For there is no absolute and undeniable *relatable* Truth. It is always hidden and has to be searched for by the individual "within" himself.

*

What we can say for certain is that once the Law is set in motion, it proliferates. *Once* the One has self-divided to become Two and together they produce Three, Four and Five, five Books of the Law are required to describe that experience and its repercussions. The process and conduct of all physical, mental and religious/ spiritual phenomena are laid down.

Laws can be taken as descriptive of how it *is* . . . or they can as interpreted and applied by the "elders" to the "sons and daughters" of the tribe, be learned as the prescribed (pre-written) code of behaviour which must be observed ("male") and obeyed ("female"). (Thus, for the Jew, the laws regulate every sphere of life from collective worship in the synagogue to family custom and ceremony to individual self-discipline).

Why should there be such Law?

84

Because, without understanding the Law, how could we make any sense whatsoever of our lives?

Imagine a situation where all law is ignored . . .

*

As we reach puberty and the sex energies arise in us, we become strongly influenced by the law of pro-creation . . . multiplication by the propagation of seed. The instinct ("female") for continuity —survival of the species—manifests in our desires. And we tend to believe that we are responsible for that survival.

This is a staggering belief or assumption.

For it suggests that we assume the fate of mankind to be in our control and keeping. If we all, universally, wanted mankind to cease—and forswore copulation—then the species would die out!

But did "God" give man such power? Because Adam did not "eat of the tree of life" are we not saved from the most inconceivable power. Are we not mercifully protected by not having the ultimate power of life/death . . . which would indeed make us as "gods"?

"But surely," it might be said, "We do have such power? We can kill . . ."

*

And Cain talked with Abel his brother: and it came to pass, when they were in the field, that Cain rose up against Abel his brother, and slew him.

(Genesis, 4: 8)

*

Is not death the greatest enigma of all (apart from birth; but birth is not so consciously immediate as the death we have to face)?

From the time that I become aware that I am, I very soon become aware that there is the possibility that I may die; and then the realisation that I am bound to die. There will come a time when I am not.

My being able to cope with the awareness of death will very

85

much depend on the influence of the society I am born into. And here there is a wide spectrum of possibilities. What I learn about it will depend on the quality, intelligence and character of what I am taught (especially the "religious" element in that teaching).

It could be inculcated into my mind that death is to be welcomed . . . as a release, perhaps, into a "better" situation than here on earth (though that may be presented as an improvement that has to be earned; otherwise it may turn out to be a "worse" situation). Or I could be influenced by an atheistic-materialistic philosophy . . . that death is just a "full stop", finish, nothing. Or, in the absence of any strong religious or pragmatic doctrine, I may find myself in an environment which ignores and avoids the issue.

If the society in which I grow up ignores and avoids the issue then I shall be ignorant of it also. If I do nothing to prepare myself for the event—and there is no one who will help me to do so— the chances are that I shall be fearful of it when I am faced with it—especially if it is my own death.

Such a situation is common enough in modern, wealthy, urban and industrial societies. Thus the emphasis is placed on longevity —the obsession with postponing the inevitable. Of course it is natural to wish to survive as long as possible, but when this becomes an end in itself, and little attempt is made to evaluate the worth of the life itself or how the ending of it might be prepared for, then the "collective psyche" of the society becomes anxious and tense. There may, for example, arise a morbid and vicarious interest in the disaster and death that befalls others.

*

The first person actually recorded as "dying" in Genesis is Adam himself, after he had lived nine hundred and thirty years. (And this is not until chapter 5, which is all about generations, ages and dying.)

Nevertheless, although nowhere does it say that he is dead, it is commonly taken that Abel's is the first death.

It is assumed that to "slay" is synonymous with killing, although the primary meaning of slay is simply "strike". Even though blood was evidently shed, there is no evidence that Abel died. And, as opposed to the word "slay" and as distinct from it, the word "kill" is not used until several verses later. (Further, in the original Hebrew, the word used derives from roots meaning approximately "overcoming with physical force".) And even then it is not known how the word "kill" originated in the English language and we therefore do not know what it originally meant, before it was taken to mean "put to death" or "deprive of life"!

In other words, we have *assumed* that we know the meaning of "slay" and "kill" even though we do not know the real meaning of "dying" and "death"!

However, that apart . . . according to the story . . . Abel does not reappear . . . so we assume him to have disappeared . . . to have been eliminated.

*

And the Lord God said unto Cain, Where is Abel thy brother? And he said, I know not: Am I my brother's keeper?

(Genesis, 4: 9)

*

If we look at this most familiar of quotations from the Pentateuch, suddenly it can begin to *sound* differently. I have always heard a sullen, murdering Cain defying the Lord God and saying, as it were, "How should I know where he is?" as he hopes to avoid detection. Apart from the fact that we only *assume* that Cain *knew* it was "wrong" to "kill", consider what a strange cry it is. "Am I my brother's keeper?" Could he not be *asking*?

And, "Where is Abel thy brother?" . . . "I know not."

He may possibly have known where Abel's *body* was . . . if we assume that he did not commit murder and bury the body (because, curiously, "The voice of my brother's blood crieth unto me from the ground").

But have you ever looked at a dead body . . . of someone you knew? The form and the substance is still recognisably there; the life or the animation has gone; there is no "consciousness" or "mind" evident; you would perhaps say, at that point, "It is so-and-so's body." But would you feel it correct to say, "It *is* so-and-so?" For you have to admit that he or she (whoever he or she was) is no longer there! He or she has "disappeared" as far as you are concerned. And if someone asked you where he or she was, would you not, with all honesty reply, "I do not know".

And you might add, in so many words, "Do I have any control over his coming into this world or his going out of it?"

Can I ever really be responsible for "taking" life any more than I can "give "it?

I may be instrumental in killing a living body . . . but have I done anything to the "life"?

*

Perhaps what we can glean from this story is that, in "striking" Abel, Cain lost his innocence (meaning, as we have said, "not hurting", for "hurt" derives from a word meaning "knock" or "strike").

And as a result of losing his innocence, the Lord punished him (by condemning him to be "a fugitive and a vagabond . . . in the earth")

*

As soon as I know "I am", I identify myself with my body. I learn from experience that bodies have a duration of life and then die. (I am committed to being a "fugitive" and "vagabond" or wanderer whilst I am here; for I have fled wherever it is that I came from and I am not going to be able to stay here forever).

The mind, therefore comes to imagine a future time when the body will die.

Therefore the mind concludes that "I am" bound to die . . . unless I can find evidence to prove that "I" continue somewhere else after death.

What is more, the mind assumes, if I kill someone else's body, "he" or "she" will die.

And as I would rather someone else does not kill me, I must be extremely circumspect about my ability to kill other people.

No one wants to be killed and does not usually want to kill. And yet . . . people kill each other . . . all through history they have done it . . . and continue to do it.

So, here we stand . . . trapped between our own birth and our own death, with the potential to take part in the creation of another life and to take part in another's death.

"I" that am born . . . can cause birth?

"I" that am bound to die . . . can cause death?

Who am I?

Where did I come from?

Where do I go to?

What *is* birth? What *is* death?

If we knew the answers, then could it not be said that we would have taken "also of the tree of life, and eat, and live for ever"?

But our forefathers did not . . .

But, if the tree is there, why should we not eat of it? We were not forbidden to do so.

It was only after eating of "the tree of the knowledge of good and evil" that Man was banished from the garden and "the way of the tree of life" was kept by "Cherubims, and a flaming sword".

Kept for whom? To keep who out?

If we found a way to retrieve our innocence and wholeness? . . .

*

Most tribes or societies impose on their young, strict instruction about hurting and killing; and institute punishment if the law in such matters is disobeyed. At root, within the society itself, such law is in the interest of the *continuity and survival of the tribe*. And the collective survival transcends individual survival for in the interest again of the former, not only may the sanctioning of the killing of members of other tribes be given but the individual is put at risk of being killed.

In a stable, wealthy, peaceful and lawful society it may be easy enough to resist the temptation to violence and the desire to kill is unlikely to arise. But the "civilised" veneer may not be all that deep.

All is well so long as I can more or less shape life to my liking without hindrance, but . . .

If, by stretching out a hand, I can pick an apple from a tree and, eating it, discover that it is delicious and satisfying, then the next time I am hungry I remember and look for another apple from that tree. The next apple I find may be higher up the tree so that I will have to make extra effort to pick it.

Now, let us suppose that all around me as I stand there beneath the tree there is grass—which could be food for me but which is not nearly so tasty as an apple. I appear to have a choice; either I eat the grass, satisfy my hunger and continue to exist; or I make extra effort to climb the tree and eat the apple, thereby not only feeding myself but also increasing the enjoyment through tasting apple instead of grass.

It seems to me that it requires certain effort to subsist; but life tends to teach me that I have to make more effort if I wish to pursue and heighten the enjoyment of sensual appetites. It seems that the greater the effort, the more likely the reward.

But what happens if, in pursuit of that reward, I have to compete and obtain it at the expense of others?

What if there is only one apple left on the tree and, just as I reach for it, someone else on the other side of the tree also puts out a hand to pick it? Can we both eat the apple?

We could *halve* the apple. But then I would only have half the satisfaction and enjoyment. What happens will depend on the intensity of my hunger and my desire to gratify my senses. If half the apple does not seem sufficient to me, then I will try to take the apple first and keep it for myself. And, if my desire is very strong, I could be provoked to strike or kill if I meet opposition from the other person. And why not? I have as much right to survive as the other person? Therefore strength must decide which of us is to have the apple? It depends on my will to shape life to suit myself.

But that law is inexorable. If I am prepared with my greater strength to kill to shape life to my liking, then I must be prepared to be killed when I meet someone stronger than myself.

Perhaps an apple on a tree may seem too trivial a reason for killing but as with the law of numbers—where 1 to 1000 is relatively insignificant compared to 0 to 1—the quantum jump is not between killing for the highest motive and killing for an apple; it is between the desire-less state of innocence and my wanting to shape life.

As soon as I want something, however noble or mean, I am open to the possibility of going to extreme lengths to obtain it; that is the law.

We may say that there is nothing we could want so much that we would kill for it . . . but are we absolutely sure? Would it not be more correct to say that there has been nothing so far in our lives that we have wanted desperately enough . . . ?

*

Do I instinctively know that it is wrong to kill?

Or have I been conditioned for so long that I do not remember that it is something that has been impressed on me through learning?

Whichever the case, I have to admit that it is possible that I may be driven to kill . . . in the interests of survival of self, family or tribe.

Could it be that the *dilemma*—"assuming two" (alternatives)—to kill or not to kill—is based both on ignorance and a fallacy?

Could it be that, although my body may be instrumental in "killing" another body, it is ignorant to believe that I can destroy *the life and spirit* in that body? The fallacy would be to assume that "I" (one) can destroy another "I" (one), "some-one-else"? (Likewise "I" cannot be destroyed by the killing or death of my body).

Thus, the crime of murder (killing for self-gain) would have quite another emphasis and implication . . . that no man has the right to shorten the natural span of physical existence of another human being, thereby depriving him of the means of completing the fulfilment of his life's purpose.

Thus the apple must be halved and shared with the other. And if there are no apples left, the grass must be shared. And according to how much grass there is, all survive or all die.

But it is not so simple as that! This materialistic, humanistic, communist ideal is only half the story.

"God" decreed that Abel was not to survive. Generation was not to be through simple division. Continuity through sharing is the "female" view. And "God" decreed that generation was to be through the "male" line (Cain) . . . until the arrival of Seth (direct from "God" himself).

The implications are enormous . . . and run through every activity of the individual, the state and mankind as a whole.

*

However, the individual is one thing . . . the survival of the collective "tribe" another. Continuity of tribe, nation, race takes precedence over survival of the individual. The laws which operate at the level of war take no account of particular human beings.

There would seem to be wars of *two* kinds (as, by now, we are perhaps beginning to expect!). There are those apparently motivated by economic survival or expansion (through multiplication) which involve extension of territory. (We could call this "female" motivation because it is associated with the physical—occupation of space, increase of land for growth of productivity, maintenance of continuity of the tribe, and so on). And there are those wars which are motivated by the desire to prove supremacy and which involve elimination by destruction of "inferior" tribes through assimilation (addition) or genocide (subtraction). (We could call this "male" motivation—like the Cain elimination of Abel to ensure the "male" line—because it is associated with abstract ideologies, religious "evangelism", the perfection of man, the destruction of "ignorant", "impure" and "impotent" strains, and so on).

It is of course difficult to separate the two because they frequently march hand in hand.

But, when it comes to ensuring the continuity of your own "line", whether it be for materialistic or idealistic reasons, and there is that which stands in the way of either the continuation or perfection of that "line" . . . what will you do?

*

And, of course, mankind itself tends to abhor wars between its members because the collective, physical body "Man" fears that which may destroy the continuity of Man himself.

And it would seem that the Abel in Man has no "future"; the Cain in him has a limited "future"; only through the Seth in him is there a meaningful and lasting "future".

*

Passing time itself—from which we get the impression of continuity—could be said to be "female" and NOW, the present impulse, is like the "male" penetration which divides time into past and future, impregnating the given moment and drawing on the substance of past memory (the "mother") produces the future possibility (the "son").

The question is . . . which of the three sons will it be?

*

Once the One divides and becomes Two is the One lost for ever?
Or is it there in every number that follows?
Numbers have properties and qualities of their own—which fascinate us and lead us to believe that they exist in their own right. But are they not all derived from and exist as functions of the One?

Once wholeness and innocence is lost and I become involved in the world, can I ever be whole and innocent again?

If I come to learn something it becomes a part of me—in memory. I may pretend to other people that I do not know it but I cannot pretend to myself. Is it possible to forget—to eliminate memory?

Or is it really a case of realising that I have assumed that the properties and qualities exist in their own right whereas, in reality, they are simply functions and projections of "I", the One upon whom they all depend?

*

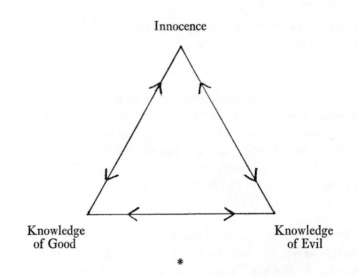

Innocence

Knowledge
of Good

Knowledge
of Evil

*

The Torah is a Hebrew word meaning "teaching".

What is the purpose of teaching?

To learn something that I do not already know?

In which case it may take me further and further away from the state of innocence.

Or is it something which may reveal to me what I already know but have not yet realised?

In which case it may lead me back to understanding the Truth.

Thus the teaching may educate me—"lead out" (of ignorance) —not by in-duction but by re-duction ("lead back again"). It will not be done by adding to "me" but by reducing or subtracting from "me".

*

Does this not suggest that innocence is a divine state from which Man fell, not as an unfortunate consequence of his wilfulness but as an inevitable and deliberate consequence of "God's" purpose as prescribed by Law?

For does not the original innocence seem barren, life-less, unconscious?

Given that One exists, does it not exist in isolation? It cannot

94

experience itself; it simply *is*. This being the case, it cannot *know* that it is. It does not have that experience.

In order to experience there must be that which witnesses the experience.

Thus One must separate from itself.

Once divided, what is there to stop continued division?

Infinity is possible.

But infinity—an in-finite, un-ending whole—is a quantum jump away from One in precisely the same measure that One is a quantum jump away from Nothing.

Mind will wrestle . . . but is there a *feeling* there?

$$\text{ABSOLUTE} \atop \text{NOTHING} \xrightarrow[\substack{\text{the division (multiplication) of} \\ \text{One}}]{\substack{\text{The un-ending mathematical Law} \\ \text{set in motion by}}} {\text{ABSOLUTE} \atop \text{EVERYTHING}}$$

What, in the final analysis, is the difference between Absolute No-thing and Absolute Every-thing?

What is the difference between zero and infinity?

Is it that zero is "before" existence and infinity "beyond" experience?

In the original *innocence* there is *no knowledge* of being.

But through *experience* of being, there can be *knowledge* of *innocence*.

*

Where did I come from?

Why do I live?

Where do I go to?

Who am I?

Only through Man's Life can such questions exist.

Only through Man's Life can such questions be answered.

The "loss of innocence" is the first lawful step on the journey to "knowledge of innocence".

Such Knowledge is Wisdom.

It is the capacity of Man, through experience of Life, to know Himself.

*

95

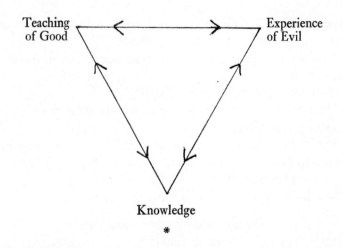

Teaching of Good   Experience of Evil

Knowledge

*

The Judaic faith depends on this law or principle.

Through the history and experience of the "people of Israel" (the *twelve* tribes being the constitution of the whole of humanity), you understand your own experience.

Through the teaching of the Law and the Prophets, that experience may be illuminated.

On both counts, the incapacity of the mind to transcend its own limitations forces an "understanding" of that which is beyond intellectual explanation ("the breaking out of the shell or covering of the mind"—the fulfilling of the Testament).

The ordinary functioning of mind cannot encompass an understanding of nothing; nor can it encompass an understanding of everything; not whilst it is involved with the world of the finite, the particular, the physical body and its island of time between birth and death.

For mind contained within the limitation of such condition, "the Lord thy God" becomes essential. It gives *form* to a *feeling*, expression to an incompleteness.

*

And to Seth, to him also there was born a son; and he called his name Enos: then began men to call upon the name of the Lord.

*

Unable to live any longer in *ignorance* (ignoring the Truth), we seek to find help.

Is it because we feel that there is something to know and understand?

We turn and seek help from those who can interpret and reveal the Law and its meaning—the Prophets.

We hope that they may be able to take us from this state:

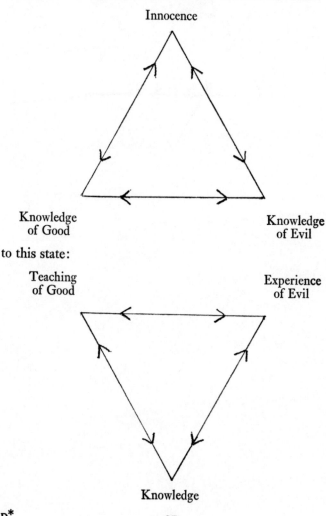

Innocence

Knowledge
of Good

Knowledge
of Evil

to this state:

Teaching
of Good

Experience
of Evil

Knowledge

so that we may understand:
"The Lord our God, the Lord is One!

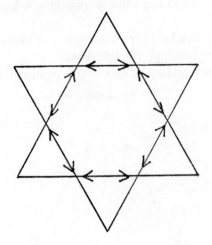

Nine

So, here we find ourselves well into a book which we have chosen
to call *The Judaic Law* . . . and there may be readers who will still
be saying to themselves, "What exactly do the foregoing chapters
have to do with Judaism?"

And if such a reader happens to be Jewish, he may well also be
saying, "This book has nothing to do with the Jewish religion
which is an integral part of my daily life. It is not relating the
orthodox Jewish faith and doctrine . . . telling what I believe . . .
describing what a Jew learns and practises in his religion."

And such comment or protestation cannot be denied.

But we, the authors, set out in our approach to Judaism (as with
the other "world" religions in the other books in this series) from
the standpoint of the "unbeliever" asking himself or herself, "What
is this religion? . . . How can this religion, as a human phenomenon,
be understood and how can it help me to understand who I am and
the purpose of my life?"

Thus, there are basic questions we can ask:

In what way is Judaism a religion?

It is generally accepted as a religion but *what does that mean*?

How is a particular religion related to the concept "religion"?

Is Judaism a system of belief peculiar and appropriate only
to a certain portion of humanity by accident of birth which
makes that portion in any *real* and *profound* way special and
privileged?

Does the Jew by virtue of his particular system of belief have
access to a revelation about himself that is denied to the rest of
mankind?

If this is so, is the rest of mankind in some way condemned

99

by the accident of its birth or should it, if it were possible, become Jewish in order to be "saved"?

Surely this is an absurd logic . . . but one that is inescapable if we take the current performance and interpretation of religion at its face value?

If we take the view that "salvation", whatever that may mean, depends on an accident of birth and environment . . . that is to say that one may be exclusively "saved" because one happens to be Jewish, Christian, Hindu, Buddhist, Muslim, or whatever . . . then we continue to sow the seeds of division.

If the ultimate salvation of mankind depends on belief in a *particular* form of faith, then heaven help us, for the prospect can only be one of continuing conflict!

Among the propositions that we are making . . . or certainly implying . . . is that belief in the particular divides and sets man against man. (We are not implying that this is "wrong"; only that it is a fact; which in turn, implies that it has a purpose—to restore unity, the One.) Thus belief in a *particular* religion exclusive of all others is self-centred and a form of discrimination which must ultimately be self-destructive.

Ecumenicism does not then lie in some kind of amalgamation of belief and practice. It is not a case of one religion emerging as superior to all others or absorbing all others into its particular ethos. It is a case of man's understanding transcending all particular forms of belief and practice . . . a case of realising the essential Truth which gave birth to religion itself, before it divided into particular religious forms . . . before those forms took on their particular "personalities". Religion itself, as a psychological phenomenon, must evolve as man himself evolves and, in so doing, throw off the "covering" which is no longer serving its protective and nurturing purpose. The "covering" or "shell" must be shed or broken through if it not to become negatively restrictive.

Once a religion has taken on a more or less crystallised form or personality it becomes exclusive and depends on attracting belief in it . . . and this it does through a mixture of threat and promise. Thus, when religion takes on particular forms of doctrine and practice, it becomes predominantly "female" and becomes primarily concerned with self-survival, continuity, expansion and propagation. On the other hand, in its "male" aspect, it is quite different in motivation. It becomes the vital means by which man can be helped to discover his own nature and purpose. And, providing it fulfils that purpose, it does not matter what form it happens to take from time to time. The purpose of the formal religion is to raise man above the support and protection of formal religion . . . to make him non-exclusively a "religious" man amongst all men.

Thus "God" is not a concept to be believed, once the mind has reached maturity; at that point the "creative-destructive" spirit in him becomes active in removing the covering of false belief (that which has been unreasonably and inappropriately taken on trust) and the mind "realises God", not as a concept but as an experience.

*

Therefore, what is the point of trying to understand what an orthodox Jew believes and does—unless you happen to be one?

That concern is exclusive to the Jew and if he chooses to believe in that particular doctrine and faith then that is his responsibility and he must abide by it whilst it provides for him the strength, comfort and protection that adherence to that particular dispensation affords him.

But how can formal Judaism help anyone who is not a Jew but who is searching for the Truth and wishes to know what, if anything, can reasonably be believed in this life?

Would it help to learn the Jewish doctrine and practise its rituals?

If the answer is negative, should we then ignore Judaism altogether?

Certainly not; for if we do so, we may miss its essential contribution.

And so what we are suggesting in this book is that we really need to examine the "roots" of Judaism (and not the "branches") in order to find the essence of the original inspiration on which the religion itself was founded. We need to find the vital message of the original teaching, not relate the performance which has become superimposed on it throughout succeeding generations.

We may hope and trust that those original scriptures may reveal the Truth to any man in a manner appropriate to the time. (The fact that thay have survived for thousands of years is hint enough that they do convey something vital). And in a way peculiar and relevant to the authors of this book, we have tried to penetrate what the written Judaic testament and tradition reveal to us. And we are hoping to convey that to us it reveals the Law—not simply as the rules by which men should regulate their behaviour (though that may be a valid disciplinary aspect of it) but as a revelation as to the function of man in the universe and how every aspect of his physical and mental experience describes, and is described by, that Law.

If that Law is truly understood . . . "God" is inevitable and undeniable.

The Law becomes not a matter of belief . . . but realisation of how *it is*. It just *is* . . . Justice.

*

And we are suggesting that such revelation or conviction arises from study and consideration of the Jewish scriptures; especially from the Torah.

So let us pause, as it were, to consider what material we are confronted with in the Pentateuch.

Two thousand years or so ago, certain stories ostensibly relating to the history of some nomadic desert people were written down in a language called Hebrew. Simply that.

The core of these recorded stories are contained in five "books".

The five books each contain, in their translated form in English, a certain number of chapters: Fifty chapters of Genesis, forty of Exodus, twenty-seven of Leviticus, thirty-six of Numbers, thirty-four of Deuteronomy. In all, then, we have one hundred and eighty-seven chapters.

And then each chapter is divided into verses and the Book of

Genesis alone contains one thousand, five hundred and thirty-three verses.

Each verse contains a number of words (the first verse of all having *ten words*) so that the total number of words involved runs into tens of thousands, in the English translation.

If we then accept that every word is sacred and has significance (for which reason, as we have said, it has been scrupulously preserved and reproduced in the scrolls since the first century before the Christian era), we will appreciate that there is wealth enough of material to satisfy years and years of study and interpretation.

So, how could we approach it? What can we hope to do?

It is understandable that we cannot do very much in so short a commentary as this book. It cannot be our hope or intention to enter in detail into the labyrinth of theological debate nor follow the repercussions of this testament on the history of a people. How could any one book such as we are writing *now* . . . and such as you are reading *now* . . . do sound justice to such a vast prospect? It is not possible.

But, as we have said, perhaps we can ask a few pertinent questions and perhaps convey a hint of what it has conveyed to us *in our experience* . . .

*

What is the point of any religion if it remains simply a historical record, or a recited doctrine, or a habitual performance? We must ask that question in relation to Judaism if we are to take even one step towards understanding it . . .

If you read the Pentateuch as a story a thousand times, or heard it read a thousand times, or studied a thousand commentaries on it, would it necessarily help you to understand, feel and know what it means to be "religious" yourself?

*

The Judaic testament is there available to any one of us should we wish to spend the time and make the effort to concentrate on it. Any one of us, NOW, may begin to read:

In the beginning God created the heaven and the earth . . . and we can continue to read, word after word, until we reach:

. . . *And in all that mighty land, and in all the great terror which Moses shewed in the sight of all Israel.*

And in between we will find that the Torah, the basis of the religion, is apparently a series of historical episodes in which the behaviour of the tribal "ancestors" (rather like the Greek gods) was by present day standards of judgement extremely violent and immoral. It is a saga of sin, punishment, destruction, killing, death, suffering, lying, deceit, licentiousness, incest, illegitimacy and so on. It is on this foundation that Judaism was apparently founded (and, perhaps paradoxically, one which Moses in a sense "disowned" and countered with his pronouncement of the commandments as a code of behaviour by which men should live.)

Apart from the proclamation of "God" himself as the source, and the concept that the "Lord is One", in what sense can this story be said to be "religious"? What can reading this "sacred" canon do for *us now*?

On the face of it, it is not an inheritance that one would expect anyone to be proud of or to be identified with. None of the key protagonists, the "holy fathers", come through it with much honour and glory. Even with their extraordinary privilege of being personally spoken to, instructed and guided by "God" himself, their achievements were highly suspect and mediocre and they frequently disobeyed and made mistakes.

Once again, on the face of it, we are surely not unreasonable in asking, "What has this strange and archaic story got to do with understanding what it means to live a religious life today?"

Is it just a case of obeying commandments which I believe came direct from "God" himself?

What is the point of that? Even Moses himself, who as the giver of that law and presumably strictly obedient to it, was not allowed to cross Jordan into the Promised Land.

Where is there any sense in it all?

Surely this is not the valid basis for religious faith?

*

Or is it perhaps that "religion" is another of those words of which we have vaguely assumed we know the meaning?

Is it rather a restricted idea that religion is only something to do with divine worship, morality, obedience, being "good", and so on? For example, in assuming that the purpose of religion is to make us "good", might there not be a danger that we will fail to see the real nature and purpose of the so-called "bad" in us? If "God" created all things, why did he create "evil"?

Surely there can be no real comprehension of being "religious" unless we are prepared to investigate every aspect of our own nature and realise why it is "good" or "evil" *in relation to what purpose*?

How can we objectively judge our own actions unless we understand the *whole* Law of creation-continuity-dissolution, or birth-life-death?

We could be said to be exposed in our upbringing to the "female" aspect of religion where the emphasis is on obedience, love, continuity, security, reassurance, comfort, service, reward. As feeble mortals born into this world it is appropriate and merciful that the testament should so protect us from so-called "evil". We could leave it at that but what about the "male" aspect of religion? In this aspect, as he "wakes up" to being the witness of the world, Man is called to understand the whole Law—to understand the purpose of righteous anger, creative destruction, punishment, evolution through dissolution, and so on. In this aspect is seen the "jealous God", the "God" of wrath and judgement; and through this is seen how the Law works, how the cycle completes itself in sacrifice and death, how it really *is* for Man in this world.

And perhaps here we begin to get a sense and feeling about the Judaic Law (which is upheld by the matriarchal influence in the home and taught by the patriarchal influence in the synagogue).

For the scriptures seem to suggest to us that we suffer not because we are bad in respect of man-invented codes of morality and convenience but because we do not obey the *whole* Law, "God's" Law, in the sense of the Law which governs all processes and relationships, some of which make us anything but secure, comfortable and reassured. It is because we ignore and fail to admit the reality of the situation that we suffer continually as, time and again, we find our attempts to establish comfort and security threatened and frustrated.

Even then the dismayed "believer" will assure himself, and others, "It is God's Will that we suffer . . ." and thereby absolve himself of any responsibility in the matter.

*

So, we perhaps begin to get a sense of the Judaic message . . . perhaps we could call it a *taste* of its *flavour* . . .

*

Consider: If I give you a piece of cake and you *eat* it you will *taste* the cake.

Otherwise, the cake is simply an object with a name. You may ask me, "What is it made of?" and I can give you the recipe—a list of all the ingredients. And you may ask, "How did you make it?" and I can tell you how the ingredients are mixed, the heat of the oven and the duration of the baking. I will, in short, be able to tell you everything *about* it—its genesis, its birth, its manifestation.

But even if I make the cake and hand it to you, it will still only be an object with a name and properties.

To experience the real worth of the cake, you will have to try eating some of it. When you have taken a bite, you will have the experience of its taste.

And you may like it . . . or dislike it.

If you like it, you may follow my recipe to make one yourself.

*

The teaching is impotent without the experience; and the experience unfulfilled without the teaching; the two must be joined for there to be any evolution. The teaching is universal, available to anyone; the experience is individual. And what comes from the interaction of the two, the interpretation, is individual.

And so we look at the Pentateuch and we relate it to our own experience; and we have touched here in these chapters our interpretation of just a few verses of the first book . . . the Book of Genesis in relation to our own genesis.

In the beginning God created . . .

You . . .

Me . . .

All the You's . . .

All the Me's . . .

NOW . . . you and me co-exist.

And we are subject to the same Law . . . once we come into existence as particular members of the multitude of human beings.

Out of the One come all the numbers, multiplying towards infinity. But it is the development of the first nine archetypal numbers only which are inevitable and in the qualities and properties of each one individually and in their relationships we may see the unfolding of our own genesis. Within each one of us the story of Adam, Eve, Cain, Abel, Seth, Enoch, Lamech, Noah and so on is enacted in the development of our bodies and minds—unbeknown to us at the time.

*

And it came to pass, when men began to multiply on the face of the earth, and daughters were born unto them,

That the sons of God saw the daughters of men that they were fair; and they took them wives of all which they chose.

And the Lord said, My spirit shall not always strive with man, for that he also is flesh: yet his days shall be an hundred and twenty years.

There were giants in the earth in those days; and also after that, when the sons of God came in unto the daughters of men, and they bare children to them, the same became mighty men which were of old, men of renown.

(Genesis, 6: 1–4)

*

How did it happen . . . for me?

How did it begin for my body? In my parents' desire?

107

Or did it begin in my mother's womb ... unbeknown to my father?

Did it begin with the birth of my body? With the first breath of life?

When did it begin for my mind? With the first impression received? Or was it with the first impression that I can now remember?

It can be said that at a certain point there was "consciousness". But was *I* conscious? Or was it that my body became "conscious" and my mind became "conscious" ... *before* I was conscious of myself?

Learning began, and hence memory. It was learned for example that the object in front of me was "a table". It was taken for granted that this is what it was—and from then onwards all similar objects were given that name by me. And so with a multitude of other things, each its separate name.

But did *I know* all these things?

Was I *conscious* of knowing anything for what it really was—as opposed to what I learned about the qualities and properties of certain forms confronting me from time to time?

Above all, before I became conscious of myself as a separate and individual being, a name was given to me. And likewise I came to believe myself to be this particular being with its certain qualities and properties, called by a certain name.

But did *I know* that that was who I was—or did I assume it?

I was conscious of being some-one—but did I know really who that *one* was?

Do I really know who I am now?

*

If *you* were to meet *me* now, would you know me?

"No," you would say.

But then we could be introduced—"led into" (each other).

At a certain "moment in time", we could learn from each other information—our names, our ages, where we live, what work we do, what interests us, what has happened to us in the past, what we hope or fear will happen in the future. We could learn much *about* ("around") each other. I could tell you "all about me" and you could tell me "all about you". We could confess to each other our innermost feelings, thoughts, hopes, fears—everything we could possibly think of.

Even though we have been led as far as possible into each other, and we could claim that we "knew each other very well"—would we *really* know each other, completely and utterly?

A moment later and there would be something new about you and something new about me which would be unknown to each other. No sooner have I taken the time to say, "I know you", and there will have been time for there to have been a development in your mind that I do not know about.

Of course, we use the phrase loosely to cover varying degrees of information we have about another person but could the phrase "I know you" ever be an absolute statement?

If you cannot see through my eyes, hear through my ears, touch with my skin, taste with my tongue, smell through my nose . . . if you cannot feel with my heart, think with my mind, experience as I experience . . . can you ever begin to *know* me?

Can *one* possibly know another *one*?

How completely can you know yourself?

What happens when you suddenly realise something about yourself?

And Adam knew Eve his wife; and she conceived, and bare Cain . . .

*

And God saw that the wickedness of man was great in the earth, and that every imagination of the thoughts of his heart was only evil continually.

(Genesis, 6: 5)

*

We think we know.

We have observed, learned, remembered . . . and we think we know . . . who and what we are and who and what others are.

109

In assuming that we can know each other, we assume that we experience alike. And why not? Physically we are similar; the structure of human bodies is the same—leaving aside the male-female differences. The senses, the limbs, most organs . . . we have them in common. And yet every person differs from every other person . . . and we disagree.

Why?

Because each person's remembered past and its interpretation is different; because each person's anticipated and *imagined* future is different.

What I remember I was like, what therefore I think I am like now, what I imagine I will be like . . . is not like your memory, thought or imagination about your-self.

It seems to be the peculiar faculty of man compared with all other creatures that he can imagine the future in abstract.

Does a seed imagine the tree that it may one day become . . . or a caterpillar imagine its imago . . . or the spawn itself as a frog . . . or the lamb itself as a sheep?

Certainly the vertebrates are able to anticipate in a given situation . . . but can they imagine or dream a future situation, in abstract?

We assume not. But we recognise the capacity in man—one which may be "evil continually".

That may not mean "evil" in the sense of "bad" as opposed to "good". Maybe "evil" did not originally have anything like the connotation that it is now given? Perhaps in our exploration we now have a hint that it may mean, for example, the "female" in the human psyche tempting the mind to think continually in terms of security, continuity and repetition in the physical world . . . so that the mind is diverted from the potential of NOW? (. . . *the sons of God saw the daughters of men that they were fair; and they took them wives of all which they chose* . . .)

The future imagined or dreamed of is of my continuity and security and, hopefully, of repeated pleasures. Is it that "evil" which lures the consciousness of being-here-now into a web of make-believe about remembered past and imagined future?

*

I do not *know* when "I" began; I do not *know* when "I" will end.

I cannot remember "I am" in the past; I can only remember "I was".

I cannot imagine "I am" in the future; I can only imagine "I will be".

I am NOW . . . or *not at all*.

And then, in one moment, once-upon-a-time, I *know* I am, here and NOW.

But . . . who is the "I" in "I am"?

Who is this "first person singular" conditioning the verb "to be"?

Who am I?

Who is "I"?

*

With the emergence of that question, a new phase in the human life begins. We could perhaps say that the "spirit of I" enters into, or is born out of, the erstwhile un-self-conscious existence. The mind which has been totally concerned with the finite and the phenomenal suddenly "casts its eye heavenwards" and, in abstract, queries the mystery of its own existence.

At this moment, "I" begins . . . as the mind *knows* the presence "I am".

*

Until this moment I am simply the product of my genesis. I have been contained within the laws of my conditioning—"my old testament".

I have acquired a load of possessions, both physical and mental (beliefs, attitudes, opinions and so on), collected indiscriminately through years of interaction with my environment. My likes and dislikes constitute the covering or habit which is my "personality". My nature interacting with my history of experience forms the quality and strength of my "public image". The character of my personality is the strength through which I express myself; through it I am capable of certain abilities and skills. (Strange that the

III

word "skill" contains the word "kill"; a skill is an ability to change the form of something—to "transform" it). But my personality can, at the same time be my weakness, because it is the means whereby I can willfully fulfil my desires. It enables me, if I use it to excess, to act selfishly . . . willing gain for myself at the expense of others.

As "I", the new individual, am "born", the substitute "I", who was simply the product of my upbringing, is eliminated or dissolved. But not permanently! That which formed that former "I", my past, is continually "standing at my shoulder" influencing me. As I begin my adolescence as an individual, I carry my history. My past conditioning is both my support and my limitation. It gives rise to all the dualistic conflict which marks the onset of puberty (reflected in both the love of my parents for their support and my resistance to them when they restrict my activity). The dual nature of my personality influences ("flows into") the beginning of adulthood . . . positively and negatively, helpfully and unhelpfully . . . both strength and weakness, advantage and disadvantage, "clean" and "unclean".

*

And God said unto Noah, The end of all flesh is come before me; for the earth is filled with violence through them; and, behold, I will destroy them with the earth . . .

And, behold, I, even I, do bring a flood of waters upon the earth, to destroy all flesh, wherein is the breath of life, from under heaven; and every thing that is in the earth shall die.

But with thee will I establish my covenant; and thou shalt come into the ark, thou, and thy sons, and thy wife, and thy sons' wives with thee.

(Genesis, 6: 13, 17, 18)

*

And the Lord said unto Noah, Come thou and all thy house into the ark; for thee have I seen righteous before me in this generation.

Of every clean beast thou shalt take to thee by sevens, the male and his female: and of beasts that are not clean by two, the male and his female.

Of fowls also of the air by sevens, the male and the female; to keep seed alive upon the face of all the earth.

For yet seven days, and I will cause it to rain upon the earth forty days and forty nights; and every living substance that I have made will I destroy from off the face of the earth.

(Genesis, 7: 1–4)

*

What is the point of my history?

It will influence me for "good" or "ill" but . . . may it not serve another purpose?

May I not through memory of the past understand the Law?

The history of the Jews or Judaism very much influences their present state; and their interpretation of the Law may have helped or hindered them as a tribe; but that is not why Judaism is a religion. Their history was no "accident"; it was inevitable; thus the point is that the history reveals the Law, *is* the Law. History is bound to reflect and reveal the Law.

The revelation born of the past is the third possibility.

God said . . . behold, I . . . even I . . . will I . . .

Father: mother: son. Present: past: future.

It all depends which of the three "I's" is conditioning, passive or active.

My past can influence me both for "good" and "ill" . . . and it can also reveal to me who "I" am.

Noah (10, One Nought) has three sons (11, One One; 12, One Two; and 13, One Three) and all of them, at the beginning of the new dispensation on earth, when all the other archetypes have been dissolved, take with them the means of reproduction (their wives).

*

The time of puberty is understandably bewildering.

I, whoever I am, seem cast adrift "on the flood of life".

113

The age of about thirteen is the time of initiation (which carries the connotation of "beginning" and the "initial"—the first letter of a person's name). The body comes to maturity and I become able to take part in the procreation of the species (not "creation" but "procreation" meaning "on *be-half*" of "creation"), through the sexual act of union with another mature body.

*

And surely your blood of your lives will I require; at the hand of every beast will I require it, and at the hand of man; at the hand of every man's brother will I require the life of man.

Whoso sheddeth man's blood, by man shall his blood be shed: for in the image of God made he man.

And you, be ye fruitful, and multiply; bring forth abundantly in the earth, and multiply therein.

(Genesis, 9: 5–7)

*

The maturity of the body and the coincidental ability of the person to be conscious of and to know his or her own existence is like a second birth.

At birth the body left the protective covering of the womb and became an individual, independent body. Now, as the body and mind mature, I grow steadily away from the protective shell of family environment and step out into the unknown of an individual and independent life. I stand alone . . . as one. And, according to my nature, I may well question not only the mystery of my coming into existence but begin to break away from the laws and rules that have regulated and conditioned my thinking and actions. All this training and discipline may have shaped what I have become; but how I will develop will depend on my ability to cope with the new energies surging through me (and which of the "three sons" becomes dominant in my psyche as time passes.)

It depends on the degree to which I may become responsible for my actions . . .

*

Perhaps we may just pause again here to consider the nature and significance of numbers which, we have suggested, actually symbolise and represent the Law and whose qualities and properties seem to underlie the history of Israel. (If our proposition is condemned as invalid, then it will still remain an extraordinary coincidence!)

As they tend to be presented to us through education, numbers seem to be simply a man-invented method of accounting quantities. Reduced to this mechanical function, it is very easy to lose entirely the richness and depth of what they can tell us as they stand for the archetypal representation of properties, qualities and relationships. They can describe so much and so accurately because they state precisely the laws which govern every life process—including you and me.

We tend to think perhaps that man arbitrarily thought of nine numbers—and then thought that there was enough for all practical purposes. They are undoubtedly useful as we use them from day to day but do we ever wonder how they came to be? If we consider them deeply, it begins to become apparent that their invention cannot possibly be "accidental". Man must have discovered them as an accurate way of describing every law and principle in a way that words could never accomplish. Words are subject to interpretation and hence confusion between people and nations; numbers are universally understood and, since they are one hundred per cent lawful, they are incorruptible. ("One is one and all alone and ever more shall be so!") There is no concept so complete and perfect as a number!

And it would seem that we only need nine archetypal numbers. For what happens then?

We start again, with a new generation, a new dispensation.

And which number is it that is called back to begin again?

One.

The numbers stop at nine. A further number is not required. If the new generation is to be initiated by One ("The Lord", or "Adam" in man's case), all the other numbers have to be withdrawn —or dissolved.

One is retained—or "saved from the flood"—but takes "within

itself" the means of regeneration (the three "sons" who are an "echo" of Cain, Abel and Seth).

In order to accomplish this, there has to be an "ark" (a "chest" or "box" implying an enclosed space, a concept represented by a circle, the symbol "o" meaning nought or nothing) to preserve the One.

(The Ark of the Testimony could therefore imply "an enclosed space, nought, containing the one witness or witness of oneness!)

So the new dispensation, the new generation of mortals on earth ("in the image of God made he man"), is secured as the ark, containing "the new father of mankind", "floats on the waters" under which all the dry land is submerged. It is not the original One itself who is saved—the One remains "in the beginning"—but a kind of image or reflection of the One as it is qualified by the "enclosing space of nought".

So the potential regeneration is based on Ten (for which the Latin word "decem" has the metonymical meaning "an indefinite number". And strangely, Noah means, "rest"—which implies both a pause and the remainder).

Noah and his three sons—One and its potential threefold development—wait to re-populate the earth as they float between earth and heaven.

*

These are the generations of Noah: Noah was a just man and perfect in his generations, and Noah walked with God.

(Genesis, 6:9)

*

There is still only the One ("God") who makes a covenant with all that follows from "the second One" and all the "other Ones" (the Patriarchs) who come after.

*

And God spake unto Noah, and to his sons with him, saying, And I, behold, I establish my covenant with you, and with your seed after you;

And with every living creature that is with you, of the fowl, of the cattle, and of every beast of the earth with you; from all that go out of the ark, to every beast of the earth.

And I will establish my covenant with you; neither shall all flesh be cut off any more by the waters of a flood; neither shall there any more be a flood to destroy the earth.

And God said, This is the token of the covenant which I make between me and you and every living creature that is with you, for perpetual generations:

I do set my bow in the cloud, and it shall be for a token of a covenant between me and the earth.

(Genesis, 9: 8–13)

Ten

Hear, O Israel; the Lord our God, the Lord is One!

*

From nowhere . . . no-where . . . now-here . . .
the One arises out of Nothing . . . the One from Nought . . .
All One, alone . . . impotent and unfulfilled . . .

Two must come after One . . . because the concept Two arises from the possibility of "two ones".

But "two ones" must be an illusion, not real, because, if there is One, there cannot be another One . . . otherwise One would not be One.

Therefore Two must be division of the One.

Two must be "two halves".

It is only through division of itself that One becomes potent.

And, we may surmise, through that division One (as One half) sees its reflection in its Other Half.

But this is still a "static" and narcissistic situation. It can only give rise to action and reaction. Something further must happen for there to be any possibility of development.

In order that One, seeing its reflection in Two, may realise itself to be the One, that realisation ("real-i-sation") must arise through a third factor.

The Three does not arise from the direct division of One into Three. And if One simply adds itself to Two, there will still only be two (One and Two).

But if One actively divides the Two, there will be three "entities" . . . not as "three ones", an impossibility . . . but "Three as One" . . . a trinity.

The Three, the "son" of the original One (the "father") and the Two (the "mother"), "returns" to the One, affirming the singularity and reality of the One ("God"). This is the threefold Atonement (at-one-ment) arising out of the illusion or duality of Two.

This is the key to the meaning of religion (from the Latin "to bind back" as "a return to a previous state after lapse or cessation or occurence of opposite state"). Religion, in whatever form, is the binding back to One . . . the return to the Absolute Cause . . . after excursion into the duality and multiplicity of physical experience (Two) and the emergence of the unifying factor (Three), the "I", which seeks re-union.

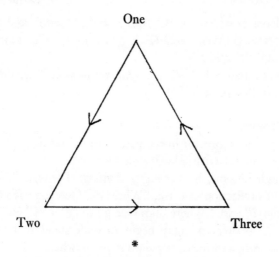

One

Two   Three

*

When is One *not* present?

Only *before* "the beginning"; before "time"; before "space"; before "coming into being".

This concept "before the beginning", "before the One", admits the possibility of Nothing. But the Judaic tradition does not noticeably concern itself with such a concept, except as a condition of the One (e.g. Ten—One Nought). Judaism begins with, "In the beginning God created the heaven and the earth."

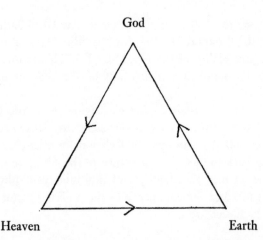

God

Heaven   Earth

(We have to wait until the Arabic cipher "zero" and the book in this series entitled *The Islamic Space* to consider more deeply the concept "Nothing").

So, rather than ask, "When is One *not* present?" we might ask: When *is* One present?

NOW.

One *is* NOW.

One cannot be present in the past or in the future.

In creation, on earth, how is One lost?

Through illusion, by becoming divided. Through "fascination with God's reflection" we ask, "Where did One come from (before "I" began)?" and, "Where does One go to (after "I" end)?"

NOW . . . perhaps we may begin to understand that One does not come from anywhere, nor does it go anywhere.

One *is* . . . nowhere . . . now–here . . . not any–where.

Two is always illusion—"in" the "play" or "game" (of living). One becomes lost "in the play".

In creation on earth, how is the illusion dispelled?

How is the "spell" of being separated from the One broken?

Through realisation of the real One ("God").

And how do we realise?

Through "knowledge" born of experience.

*

The Law of One-Two-Three is ever-present in creation, pro-
creation, and dissolution or resolution.

In every process the One and Two are usually evident enough
as active-passive forces, energy-matter, "father-mother" and so on.
And Three, as the resultant, can sometimes be easily appreciated.

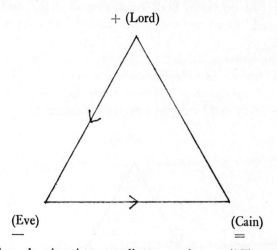

+ (Lord)

(Eve)   (Cain)
—   =

And then the situation complicates as the possibility arises for
that which was active to become passive and that which was
passive to become active.

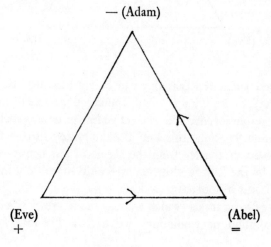

— (Adam)

(Eve)   (Abel)
+   =

The resultant "offspring" is then of a different nature.

These two alternatives arising from One and Two being either active or passive we have suggested as being represented, for example, by Cain ("gotten . . . for the Lord") and Abel ("she again bare his brother").

These two offspring, both resolutions of active and passive, are "neutral" which means "neither the active first nor the passive second".

But the situation is further complicated by the fact that the third, the neutral, factor can become the condition of the relationship of the other two—a "third force" in fact—and one which is far more subtle and harder to perceive in experience.

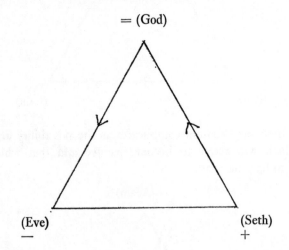

= (God)

(Eve)
—

(Seth)
+

We have suggested that this can be seen as the case with the "third son", Seth ("God . . . hath appointed me a seed") where the result or resolution becomes the active line of development.

We cannot continue this line of enquiry any further for it will surely divert us too far from the theme of our book—religion as revealed by the Law (and it may well only appeal to a minority of readers!). But it does seem (at least to us, the authors) that within these three basic triads (which we may see as creation, procreation and dissolution or resolution) we have a five-fold foundation (involving the first "family" of five "persons"—Adam, Eve, Cain, Abel and Seth) whose relationships give the quality and property of the nine archetypal numbers (One-Two-Three, Four-Five-Six, Seven-Eight-Nine). And all of it depends and stems from the force carried by the original One—whether "God" is active, passive or conditioning in any given moment, NOW.

*

Time is One—existing "unknown".
Time is divided into Two—past and future—existing "unknown".
Out of the Two arises the third factor, NOW—existence known.
NOW reveals the duality of "known" past (memory/Eden) and "known" future (imagination/Promised Land).
Only NOW can One "know" the past.
Only NOW can One "know" the future.
Only NOW can One "know" the present.
(Otherwise One is "lost" in remembering the past and imagining the future).
Only NOW can One "know" the Oneness of All . . . the *presence* of "God".
NOW and KNOW are almost synonymous . . . just the effect of a "silent" K makes them distinct.

*

"K"—the eleventh (One-One) "sound symbol" of the Hebrew and English alphabet . . . the Semetic symbol *Kaph* originally being like a "K" in reverse . . . three lines, two of them forming an angle whose point touches the third, an upright vertical line, a "one" . . . its sound is that of a "back voiceless stop" . . . used in astronomy to designate a constant "the square of which is a measure of the mass of the sun" . . . if "J" is not reckoned as a number of the series (being considered a form of "I"), "K" is the tenth (One-Nought) member . . .

We may now begin to feel an understanding as to how law and number underlie the form of sound, letter and word . . . which in turn allows us to communicate experience. The teaching (of the "ancient law") acting on our experience in life enables One to understand . . . One-Self.

*

Try pronouncing the word "NOW" aloud.

Note the interplay of active, passive, result and condition . . .

The negative "N" forms as the tongue blocks the vibrating sound in the throat before releasing it into the cavity of the mouth where the enclosing space of "nothing" gives rounded form to the "O" before the two lips close and almost encompass the passing sound, channelling the current of breath as it leaves in the "W".

Now . . . try pronouncing "ONE". The interplay of forces change order as the almost closed lips condition the issuing sound, then withdrew to permit the full mouth cavity expression of the "O" before the tongue curtails the sound in "N".

In "NOW" it is as if the negative resistance of "N" gives "birth" to the space of "O"; whilst in "ONE" it is as if "N" is the "death" or resolution of it.

*

We make no apology for emphasising the sound of words . . . as opposed to investigating the more usual lingustic and etymological origins and derivations.

The disciplines of the latter, as they compare *written* languages and trace words back through history, provide useful information about inter-relationship of tribes in chronological time. But they do not take the enquirer back to the original sound and what it meant to the first man who spoke it. Tracing back through history never reveals the first cause; rather is history always the result of hidden causes. The cause is never evident in memory, nor in imagination; which concern themselves with effects.

The only possibility of really understanding sound—and its formation into words—is by sounding and listening NOW. Only then may the Law be revealed (as the numerical Law which dictates sequence, pitch, vibration frequency, harmony, and so on). Only NOW will we understand and witness the Law. (Thus it is that tracing the history of Judaism—its effects in time past—will not reveal its true meaning as a religion. We can only do that by discovering how it can cause revelation of our present experience.)

The Hebrew script has twenty-two consonants and they were written down from right to left with no word breaks, punctuation nor other "guidance". The vowel sounds had to be (and still are) "breathed into" the symbols in order for there to be verbal expression (as nouns need verbs to "bring them to life"). It was for each witness of the Law to "inspire" and be inspired through vocal expression of the scripture. (The Oral Law in Judaism was derived from the Written Law and spoken by, for example, the Prophets).

In terms of human sound and the laws which govern its formation and expression, there can only be "one original language" (all human beings have the same vocal mechanism—one throat, one mouth, one tongue, two lips, etc.).

And the way back to the one, original language is not through trying to trace back through the multitude of languages to a historical origin but by listening to the sound NOW.

*

And the whole earth was of one language, and of one speech . . .

And the Lord said, Behold, the people is one, and they have all one language; and this they begin to do: and now nothing will be restrained from them, which they have imagined to do.

Go to, let us go down, and there confound their language, that they may not understand one another's speech.

So the Lord scattered them abroad from thence upon the face of all the earth: and they left off to build the city.

Therefore is the name of it called Babel; because the Lord did there confound the language of all the earth: and from thence did the Lord scatter them abroad upon the face of all the earth.

(Genesis, II:I, 6–9)

*

. . . and now nothing will be restrained from them, which they have imagined to do . . .

And so, at puberty, "I" begin to become individual and independent.

(Though in fact, in doing so I become particular, separate and dependent on many things!).

And though I have learned the language of my tribe—and may be learning other languages as well—I find, if I ask, that no one can tell me the Truth.

Who can tell me Truth?

What language will they use?

Who can answer the deep questions in my mind in a language I can understand?

Who can tell me who I am?

There is no human language whose words can describe the inner meaning of my experience. You and I cannot tell each other the scent of flowers, the taste of an apple, the degree of joy, the depth of sorrow . . .

The language of One remains hidden within me . . . and I cannot hear it nor express it . . . until "God speaks to me" and I hear the language "without words".

*

And Noah began to be an husbandman, and he planted a vineyard:

And he drank of the wine, and was drunken; and he was uncovered within his tent.

And Ham, the father of Canaan, saw the nakedness of his father, and told his two brethren without.

And Shem and Japheth took a garment, and laid it upon both their shoulders, and went backward, and covered the nakedness of their father; and their faces were backward, and they saw not their father's nakedness.

And Noah awoke from his wine, and knew what his younger son had done unto him.

And he said, Cursed be Canaan; a servant of servants shall he be unto his brethren.

And he said, Blessed be the Lord God of Shem; and Canaan shall be his servant.

God shall enlarge Japheth, and he shall dwell in the tents of Shem; and Canaan shall be his servant.

(Genesis, 9: 20–27)

*

"I" step out onto the dry land. The "ark of my past" is left behind—the "nothing" out of which "I" now emerge.

And the three sons represent the three lines along which I may now proceed.

What a strange story to follow the emergence from the ark!

*

Shem, Ham, Japheth—begotten by Noah.

Supposing they are the natural progression from Ten (One-Nought), being Eleven (One-One), Twelve (One-Two) and Thirteen (One-Three).

Noah has too much wine ("loses sense of himself") and lies uncovered ("One with Nothing").

Ham ("father of Canaan", the "younger" son, i.e. not the youngest but younger than Japheth, "the elder") sees his father's nakedness. If Ham is One-Two, the Two may give us the clue for Eve (Two) revealed the nakedness of Adam (One); and was also the mother of "Cain".

For his unfortunate—and, apparently, unpremeditated— indiscretion Ham is cursed and Canaan is condemned to servitude—as we might anticipate as his "line of generation" will be "female" as an even number multiplying through division ("cursed" because, although mechanical division fulfils the desire for continuity, there is no hope of eventually reaching the infinite. Progression in that direction is bound for ever to the ever-receding finite, the material or maternal). The only hope for the "female" line is through having to serve, or surrender to the "male" line.

So, Noah is angry at having been seen "naked" by the "female son". On the other hand, Shem and Japheth—One-One and One-Three—are both "male" (odd). Being both of the "male" line (One and Three) they both have the means to cover, overlay or duplicate, the One. And they "go in backward" which has the (negative) connotation of not being "attracted forward" as opposites are to each other. Significantly, they do not see the "nakedness" of the One for, as we might say, "the One is behind them" as One-One and One-Three.

Japheth, the elder, as One with *Three*, carries the threefold potential for "enlargement"—although he is bound to "dwell" under the authority of the One, as symbolised by the One-One of Shem. Japheth is committed to the rise of the Gentiles (Genesis, 10:5)—the proliferation of "every *one* after his tongue, after their families, in their nations". (The idea expressed here, of multiplying "away from the One" being perhaps the origin of the association of thirteen with misfortune).

It is through Shem (the One facing the reflection of himself, One-One) that the pure "Semetic" line descends, as his generations lead through to Terah, the father of Abram.

*

The three "sons" emergence in my psyche in my adolescence.

We could say that the "future" will be based on a threefold motivation—firstly the "son Ham" (passive Canaan) concerned with continuity, security, service, repetition of past comfort and pleasure; secondly the "son Japheth" (active, Gentile) concerned with advance, adventure, increase, enlargement, seeking for advantage and gain for myself in the eyes of the world; and thirdly the "son Shem" (conditional, neutral, Semetic) concerned with the search for Truth, for understanding, for "God", for wholeness and unity, for "knowing who I am". (In other words, these three represent "body", "mind" and "spirit".)

(This, of course, has nothing to do with the present labels such as "Jew" and "Gentile". On the contrary, the Jew in the physical sense, is as likely to look for "security" and "enlargement" as anyone else, since he inevitably has the three "sons" within him).

*

We now move on to the next "quantum jump"—from one "real"

number to the next, as opposed to the "generations" that a particular number can "beget" by multiplication.

The sons of Terah (strangely, an anagram of "earth"—as if we are now "down to earth" or the physical) are again three—Abram, Nahor and Haran.

From this point onwards, the geneology becomes even more complicated as these three lines of generation, and the forces they represent, "spread out into all lands" and become "weaker" as they proliferate further and further away from the original One. (Just as numbers become more complicated as they carry various possible factorisations within them).

*

And Terah lived seventy years, and begat Abram, Nahor and Haran. Now these are the generations of Terah: Terah begat Abram, Nahor, and Haran; and Haran begat Lot.

(Genesis, II: 26, 27)

*

Thus Abram is born of the "neutral" line of Shem—with the other two sons, Nahor and Haran, to complete the triad of "forces".

And the days of Terah were two hundred and five years: and Terah dies in Haran.

Before touching on what Abram may represent in each of us, consider these three sons and their fate:

Haran dies before his father, Terah (whose father is named Nahor), in the land of his nativity.

Nahor takes as his wife his brother Haran's daughter—thus, his own niece.

Abram takes for his wife Sarai, who is his half-sister (she is the daughter of Terah but not the daughter of Terah's wife. (Genesis, 20: 12) But she is barren and "had no child".

The family, led by their father Terah, leave the place of their conception (Ur of the Chaldees) "to go into the land of Canaan" (previously cursed by Noah); "and they came unto Haran and dwelt there".

E*   129

Unto Haran . . . who is already dead?

And the days of Terah were two hundred and five years: and Terah died in Haran.

The father dying in the already-dead son?

As we progress through the chapters the names of men and places start to become the same.

As I start to become established in the world and occupy a particular place of my own, especially when I come to establish a home, that place becomes "synonymous" with me. People who know me do not say, "Let's go to such-and-such a place"; they say "Let's go to so-and-so's", giving my name as the occupant of the place.

But perhaps that is not the depth of the significance. Perhaps it is to do with the increasing density and complexity of the Law as its first principles become applied to space, form and location—especially land and property—just as, in our adolescence, we become more and more identified with our belongings.

Thus it helps to establish someone by knowing where they live, where they go to school, where they work, where they come from . . .

*

And Abram took Sarai his wife, and Lot his brother's son, and all their substance that they had gathered, and the souls that they had gotten in Haran; and they went forth to go into the land of Canaan; and into the land of Canaan they came.

(Genesis, 12: 5)

*

As I enter adolescence, the profound questions arise out of my being conscious of myself as an individual entity.

I know I am.

But who am I?

Who is the "I" who is?

No one can tell me.

I do not *know*.

But, whoever the "I" is, from now on that "I" is the father of all my endeavour—the Abram in me.

*

Terah gives birth to Abram, as a direct descendent of Shem, Noah, Seth, Adam.

But Abram's wife is barren. So she, who is also his half-sister, persuades Abram to take her maid, Hagar, "the Egyptian". He "goes in unto her" and she conceives their "illigitimate" son Ishmael.

*

And Sarai said unto Abram, My wrong be upon thee: I have given my maid into thy bosom; and when she saw that she had conceived, I was despised in her eyes: the Lord judge between me and thee.

(Genesis, 16: 5)

*

As I begin to take my place in the world, there seem to be no absolute answers to my questions.

I have no option it seems but to get on with following the ways of the world and establishing my place in it, according to the circumstances I happen to be in and the opportunities that happen to arise. I discover that wealth is the basis of mundane power and that my ambitions and future prospects are very much governed by factors outside my control. To a considerable degree the route that I follow is mapped out for me and the options open are dictated to me by others. Although the possibilities in life ahead seem to be many, I may become aware that in many respects my fate is already sealed. Apart from the limitations set by my economic situation, no matter what I may be able to be and do, the type of person I am is already established.

And so begin my "wanderings"—my successes and failures, my joys and sufferings, my "famines" and "times of plenty"—as an increasingly independent individual.

My hopes are usually in terms of gain and my fears in terms of loss.

The more I assimilate and own (note our three letters again—N-O-W, in different order), the greater my vulnerability to loss.

And the greatest "loss" of all would be the life that I think is mine.

The tendency is for my endeavour to be dominantly "female", being directed towards continuity and security of the body and establishing my place and economic status in the world. And the older I become the greater the strength of the desire to continue the life and maintain the position (the desire being linked to the fear of loss). Thus our understanding of Judaism as portrayed in the Torah becomes more poignant after Abram is told "Get thee out of thy country . . ." and he begins his journey in foreign lands. Up until that time, survival has not been a problem (just as the child in the security of his home tends not to be aware of such problems). But from then onwards, the journey of the children of Israel is motivated by a continual search for a place where they can live in peace and plenty—a land where they can establish their tribal home and raise crops and herds and feed themselves.

And so it is with us as we leave the family home, "the land of our nativity".

Why does the Law dictate that we must leave that security?

Because we shall never realise the full potential of our individuality (our "maleness") if we remain within the shell or covering of our family ("female") context.

*

And Abram passed through the land unto the place of Sichem, unto the plain of Moreh. And the Canaanite was then in the land.

And the Lord appeared unto Abram, and said, Unto thy seed will I give this land: and there builded he an altar unto the Lord, who appeared unto him.

And he removed from thence unto a mountain on the east of Beth-el, and pitched his tent, having Beth-el on the west, and Hai on the east: and there he builded an altar unto the Lord, and called upon the name of the Lord.

And Abram journeyed, going on still towards the south.

And there was a famine in the land: and Abram went down into Egypt to sojourn there; for the famine was grievous in the land.

(Genesis, 12: 6–10)

*

The first mention of Egypt.

Today, as more is discovered and appreciated about Egypt's contribution to the ancient world, the evidence suggests that its civilisation was very advanced, not only on a social, cultural and economic level but also on what we may refer to here as a philosophic, religious and spiritual level.

This visit of Abram's was of short duration; later Abraham's great-grandson, Jacob, was to lead the whole of his people once more into Egypt.

So what may this excursion into such a formidable "foreign land" imply?

What seems important to note is that the going south into Egypt is promoted by "famine"; they went there to obtain the means for survival, to find that which was essential to life and living.

(And we should note that Jesus—the founder of Christianity, an off-shoot of Judaism—was also taken as a child to Egypt in order that he should survive. There must surely be some significance in this? Why is so little made of it in Christianity? After all, Jesus was there during very impressionable and formative years . . . And we should perhaps also remind ourselves that the male line of descent to Jesus traces back (Luke, 3: 23–38), "as was supposed", seventy-six generations, through Abraham, Sem (Shem), Noe (Noah), Enos, Seth and Adam to God. He was the seventy-seventh son.)

The word "famine" (from Latin "*fames*") means hunger and the word "hunger" is defined as "uneasy sensation, exhausted condition, caused by want of food; strong desire . . ."

This "uneasy sensation" of lacking may be seen as hunger at a mental as well as a physical level (in fact, all experience of hunger is registered in the mind whether the lacking be of physical or mental food).

The "strong desire" is to be *whole* and complete.

133

And to be "whole", a complete One, is not to be deficient or divided.

To be truly individual is to be indivisible.

Thus, when I leave the security of the family home, "the land of my nativity", and venture into the world, I experience hunger. In many respects, I begin the search for wholeness and completeness. And in that interest I seek out the knowledge which will enable me to do it.

*

Of course, my body needs a certain amount of food and it requires warmth and shelter. I can grow food and build a dwelling if I have the land to do so; if not, I can learn a skill which will enable me to buy my physical requirements.

Given reasonable conditions, and willingness to work, it is not difficult to survive and satisfy at the physical level.

But how about the mental level?

Because physical survival naturally takes priority, the tendency is that the "wisdom of the world" will influence me to see complete-ness and fulfilment mainly in material terms. The tendency is to suggest that completeness and wholeness can be attained by "expansion" (by the "Japheth-Gentile" dispensation of "enlarge-ment").

But is that enough?

It is fair enough for the mind to exercise itself in the interests of my survival and that of my tribe; and even to provide against the possibility of future famine.

But supposing increased productivity and "expansion" becomes an end in itself? Supposing that is my society's "religion"?

Is it possible to reach invulnerable completeness and wholeness in that direction alone? Where does it lead to?

By eating more and more we cannot guarantee increased longevity. If we had enough food to last for ever, we would not become immor-tal!

So, though my body may be satisfied and "complete", will my mind be satisfied in the direction of continuous increase?

134

If I learned all the world's wisdom and saturated myself in its culture, would *I* become complete and whole?

If so, then I will happily stay "in Egypt" . . .

*

We have seen that numerically the direction of increase—multiplication through division—takes us further and further from the original One.

If One is *whole* (because everything that follows from it is contained within it), then the only way to regain wholeness is through return to the One.

In other words, the mind will never find satisfaction through increasing its "content" of learning, filling itself with more and more "food". It can only do so through the knowledge and understanding of One, the realisation of Unity.

"I" can never find satisfaction in believing "I" am any particular and separate "thing"; only in realising that the "I" is One. "I" cannot be increased or added to; "I" only have to surrender or subtract all things that "I" am not. Then only "I" remain—One realising One-Self.

(Thus the Israelite "leaves bondage", the Hindu "removes the sheaths of illusion", the Christian "gives up all that he hath" and becomes "poor in spirit", just as the ancient Greek obeyed the Delphic dictums, "Nothing in excess" and "Know Thyself").

*

In Judaism, religion arises directly from experience of life.

If "things" in life are going well for us we are more likely to be content. And the more content we are, the less likely we will be to seek the answers to our deepest questions. We are less likely to remember and hear the questions. But through experience in life we will learn that such contentment never lasts.

Thus, if we rely only on the provisions of the world no matter how noble and well-intentioned, we are still vulnerable to doubt and fear . . . to suffering.

135

And that suffering is a reminder . . . that we must return to One ("God") . . . *in this life* . . . and we should begin the journey NOW.

*

Abram is the "father" in each of us—the "I" who sets out to take an individual place in the world after leaving the homeland.

At first, his wife is barren so that she is incapable of motherhood (unless by the divine intervention of "God"). Hence it is not that Abram is impotent, any more than I am as I emerge out of adolescence. It is rather that I do not yet "know my own mind". Effectively, my own "wife" is not yet fertile enough for my adult and mature will to exert itself in original and independent, individual and non-derivative, thought and action. Only later will my mind mature to the potential when I can really "be myself".

Meanwhile, since I am not impotent, I can certainly be wilful!

I am willing to test my strength on the world around me.

*

Now Sarai Abram's wife bare him no children: and she had an handmaid, an Egyptian, whose name was Hagar.

And Sarai said unto Abram, Behold now, the Lord hath restrained me from bearing: I pray thee, go in unto my maid; it may be that I may obtain children by her. And Abram harkened to the voice of Sarai.

And Sarai Abram's wife took Hagar her maid the Egyptian, after Abram had dwelt ten years in the land of Canaan, and gave her to her husband Abram to be his wife.

(Genesis, 16: 1–3)

*

Out of this intercourse is born an "illegitimate son", who is to be called Ishmael. And "the angel of the Lord" tells Hagar that *he will be a wild man; his hand will be against every man, and every man's against him; and he shall dwell in the presence of all his brethren.*

136

Would this not be a fair description of wilfulness and its effect?

*

There is much in this text that we cannot elaborate on here. But the main point would seem to be that "I", as Abram, exert my will first on "the Egyptian", whatever of the world presents itself to me.

And the offspring is a "bastard I"—not the real "I", the "male" heir—but a substitute, a "pretender to the throne" (of reality or royalty), the ego.

That "I" speaks in my name through my wilfulness . . . but it is not the real "I" . . .

*

Has Abram "sinned" in the eyes of the Lord?

Apparently not; for at the beginning of the next chapter (seventeen, One-Seven; after the Hagar episode in sixteen, One-Six), we find the Lord making a covenant with Abram—and a very significant covenant at that. Abram's name is to be changed.

*

And when Abram was ninety years old and nine, the Lord appeared to Abram, and said unto him, I am the Almighty God; walk before me, and be thou perfect.

And I will make my covenant between me and thee, and will multiply thee exceedingly.

And Abram fell on his face: and God talked with him, saying,

As for me, behold, my covenant is with thee, and thou shalt be a father of many nations.

Neither shall thy name any more be called Abram, but thy name shall be Abraham; for a father of many nations have I made thee.

And I will make thee exceeding fruitful, and I will make nations of thee, and kings shall come out of thee.

And I will establish my covenant between me and thee and thy seed after thee in their generations for an everlasting covenant, to be a God unto thee, and to thy seed after thee.

And I will give unto thee, and to thy seed after thee, the land wherein thou art a stranger, all the land of Canaan, for an everlasting possession; and I will be their God.

And God said unto Abraham, Thou shalt keep my covenant therefore, thou, and thy seed after thee in their generations.

This is my covenant, which ye shall keep, between me and you and thy seed after thee; Every man child among you shall be circumcised.

(Genesis, 17: 1–10)

*

Verse *One*: . . . I am the Almighty God . . . be thou perfect;

Verse *Two*: . . . I . . . will multiply thee exceedingly . . .;

Verse *Three*: . . . God talked with him . . . ;

Verse *Four*: . . . thou shalt be a father of many nations;

Verse *Five*: . . . thy name shall be Abraham . . . ;

Verse *Six*: . . . I will make thee exceeding fruitful . . . ;

Verse *Seven*: . . . I will . . . between thee and me . . . to be a God unto thee . . . ;

Verse *Eight*: . . . the land wherein thou art a stranger . . . ;

Verse *Nine*: . . . God said . . . Thou . . . and thy seed after thee in their generations;

Verse *Ten*: . . . Every man child . . . circumcised (an encircling "nought" cut round the phallic "one". The One "unsheathed" to scatter the "seed" through generations).

*

At about twenty-one I am on the threshold of adulthood. I am now at the age of maturity when I am expected to be fully responsible for myself.

The "I" who now becomes potential father of a family is one who directs his will and begins his individual career. I start to become what I really am. I come "into my own", "in my own right"; I speak and act "in my own name".

"I" am now he who is expected to have charge of the destiny of this life.

There are plenty of problems ahead! Apart from anything else, there will be a prolonged "bondage in Egypt" (out of which the "Moses" within will lead me).

But with "the breathing of 'ah' into my name", it is now well and truly my own responsibility which will count.

Eleven

What does the introduction of the letters "a" and "h" signify (not only into Abr-ah-am but taking the place of "i" in Sarai to give Sar-ah)? Apart from accompanying the covenant with Abraham, it gives Sarai who was barren the potential to be *a mother of nations; kings of people shall be of her*; and later to be the mother of the one to be next in male line, Isaac.

"H"—the eighth letter of the Semetic, Roman, English alphabet . . . its power is that of a simple aspiration of breathing . . . the most natural sound of the body . . . drawn as a letter with three lines, two upright and one horizontal . . . two "ones" joined by one line . . .

Where does the breath come from? Where does the breath go to?

$$| \overline{\underline{\text{breath}}} |$$

"A"—the first letter . . . the first vowel . . . drawn as a letter with three lines . . .

The breath carrying the first uttered sound . . .

*

All sounds are carried on air.

The only possibility of "dead" or absolute silence is in an airless vacuum . . . a kind of "breathless void".

Thus, for human speech, all sounds are carried on breath being exhaled from the body.

The breath, however, is almost silent and there is no meaningful sound unless it activates the vocal mechanism. We may breathe silently; all that is required is that the throat and the mouth (or nose) should be "open".

Breath means life.

To live we must breathe.

When we no longer breathe, we are dead . . . no br-eath, d-eath.

A life is an expression of existence.

A life may be likened to a sound . . . almost as if the sum total of your life may be summed up in the "sound" you make during your life.

Breath is to sound as Nothing is to One.

Nothing is to One as breath is to life. And One is to Nothing as life is to death.

Thus the breath carrying sound is like no-thing being expressed as some-thing.

Sound is some-thing expressed . . . expressing one-self . . . self-expression.

Sound carries knowledge . . . and the mouth gives it form. And the knowledge is in the form of information (in-form-ation).

The voi-ce is expressed through the voi-d.

"*And God said . . .*"

*

Now breath may require "some-thing" to breathe it—but the "thing" does not explain the breath. The "thing" always requires breath in order to live. To live it must have breath "breathed into it" before it can express sound.

And the most "open" (least affected or restricted) sound that the human voice may express is the sound "ah".

Try it.

To sound "ah" we breathe inwards and then express outwards with the mouth open—the throat wide, the tongue flat and the lips apart.

It is the "first" sound, the primary vowel.

To sound "ah", we exhale the breath and will the sound into it. The sound is created and given form through us.

*

Where does the idea of the sound come from?

That is as difficult to answer as, "Where does life come from?".
It is as difficult to answer as, "Where do I come from?"

Abram was given the sound by "God".

As "life" was breathed into him", he became Abraham . . .
"father of many nations".

And Sarai also, transformed by the same gift, ceased to be barren
to become "mother of many nations".

*

What can such a story mean?

What can it mean to *me*?

Strangely enough, the "primitive" sounds of a language are the
least affected and restricted and carry a wealth of emotional expression.

"Ah" has no limiting consonant to make it a verb or a noun in
a particular language; but as a *sound* we express it often.

It is for example the sound we make when we *realise* something.

"Ah!" . . . now I understand! . . . now I see!

It is the sound we might well make when a revealing and important idea comes to mind.

"Ah!"

It is the sound immediately after *inspiration*.

To "inspire" means literally "to breathe or blow into"; and is
this not a good description as to how an idea "comes to mind"?
We might well feel that the idea has been "breathed in" or "blown in".

From whence the idea has come we may later attempt to work out
logically by tracing back through the experience which preceeded it,
hoping to find the "cause" of its "birth". And certainly we may find
much information and material or matter which was the essential
ground or "mother" of its being able to manifest itself. But the
"instant" conception and emergence of the idea before it became
formalised in thought and became comprehensible and meaningful
is a mystery. The "father", as it were, of the idea is "hidden" and,
as it emerges after its gestation in the dark "womb" of the mind,
it seems to come from *nowhere*.

When we are inspired and illuminated by an idea, it happens suddenly . . . *now-here*.

*

The sexual act, as we have already stated, is the means employed (through the union of "two halves") to pro-create the species. Each "one" of us has been procreated for and on be-half of the species.

And as such we may live out our allotted "life" obedient to the laws of passing (body) time—the laws of growing, maintaining and declining. Our life may not be inspired (and we may live as Abram, Sarai, Hagar and Ishmael). We will remain simply a tiny part of the life of the earth—like a tiny corpuscle in the life-blood or as one minute drop of dew in the oceans of water.

But within each of us, regardless of background, education and circumstance, there lies the *potential* for inspiration through the return to, and communion with, the greatest intelligence . . . the One from which All originated.

It depends on the sounds we listen to . . . and the sounds we utter.

*

This is not some high-flying hypothesis, far from it. It is something of which we have all had experience . . . and which we have implied and referred to several times in this book.

It is not complicated and sophisticated . . . only to be attained by the clever, the privileged and the "wealthy".

It is *simple*.

("Simple" derives from Latin words meaning "onefold", "once", "at once", "one by one"; and by definition it means "not compound, consisting of one element, all of one kind, involving only one operation or power, not divided into parts, not analysable").

To be "simple" means to be unified as One . . . a virtue devoutly to be wished for!

Such "simple" experience and knowledge is "felt" through "the longing and intelligence of the heart" and always has connotations of completeness, wholeness, peace, stability . . .

143

The song of a bird, the scent of a flower, the caress of a loved one, the glory of the rising or setting sun, the breath of wind on the face . . . a thousand thousand things on a list that is endless and individual . . . can transform our incompleteness and separation to well-being and wholeness. All the tensions of division are dissolved or resolved in the blissful moment as we escape the duality of remembered past and imagined future. From such simple beginnings . . . we start to find the way back to One.

This is the hint of One . . . the silent voice in the void calling us "back to Eden" or urging us to "go *up* into the Promised Land".

For a moment, we may say, "We come to our self" . . . we are here, now.

*

And they rose up early in the morning, and gat them up into the top of the mountain, saying, Lo, we be here, and will go up unto the place which the Lord hath promised: for we have sinned.

(Numbers, 14: 40)

*

The moment of orgasm is in the moment NOW . . . whether it be physical, mental or spiritual "separateness" that is resolved in that "timeless" moment of bliss.

The moment of the inspired idea is in the "timeless" moment. NOW.

The moment of inspiration is creative; the time of work before the inspiration is procreative, as is the application of the idea after the inspiration.

Thus, the One is the creative inspiration as it acts through Two to give rise to the generations of all numbers as they spread out in the direction of the ultimate, unattainable, finite number.

The One is the origin, life and breath of All. Any number, now and always depends on One.

Thus, the way to wholeness and peace can never be through travelling in the direction of the ultimate finite number—death.

144

It must be through going back towards the beginning ... and through our history understanding our origin, NOW.

*

Sound is NOW.

You cannot hear sound in the past nor in the future ... whenever you hear a sound, it is present.

And God said ...

The moment of the "living" sound is creative (or destructive, depending on whether the "God of Love" or "God of Wrath" is appropriate) and it is "male". That which gives rise to the sound, forms and holds the sound, continues the sound, is procreative and is the "female". Thus in any word-form, whatever the language, it is the sound that is the creative-destructive inspiration.

*

And the Lord said, Behold, the people is one, and they have all one language; and this they begin to do: and now nothing will be restrained from them, which they have imagined to do.

Go to, let us go down, and there confound their language, that they may not understand one another's speech.

(Genesis, 11: 6, 7)

*

The human voice ...

states, ignores, denies, praises, criticises, defies, repents, justifies, protests, condemns, encourages, divides, reconciles, provokes. sympathises, consoles, regrets, accuses, proclaims, propounds ...

carrying with it the forces of creativity, destruction, sustenance, continuity, dissolution, resolution ...

all of it—whether the speaker be aware of it or not—proclaims the inevitable affirmation: that All things originate, depend on and return to One ... the ultimate Atonement.

Hear, O Israel; the Lord our God, the Lord is One!

*

For feeling to be voiced, it is carried by the breath from the "heart" and is expressed through sound. To understand one another —really to understand—we must speak "the one language of the people who are one". We must transcend the confusion of word meaning—from which stems all division and conflict—and listen to the sound of the voice. We must speak "heart to heart".

In the Pentateuch, there are many stories of God "talking" to certain mortals. What can this mean? Does it mean an actual voice speaking audibly to be heard by the physical ear . . . or does it mean an "inner voice" being understood in the "heart"?

*

If I am not "inspired", I will be barren to the possibility of deeply revealing thought. That does not mean that I will not think —far from it; I will be thinking all the time . . . the constant repetitive thinking evolved through my conditioning, my acquired learning and adopted beliefs. I will be "enslaved" by my circum-stances and the "bondage" of the way I have been taught to think. Being a product of my past and just a reaction to the world around me, "I" become Ishmael, the son of Abram's consorting with Hagar, the Egyptian. (Nevertheless, Ishmael is blessed by God and multiplies, having "twelve princes" as sons. As Ishmael, "I" can still be useful and fruitful in the world's affairs).

But if "I" am inspired . . . becoming "original" and a trans-formed individual . . . then a whole, new potential arises . . . for understanding "God's" purpose and hence the purpose of my life. Then "I" follow the "male" line and become the true heir, Isaac, a son "born of inspiration".

*

But then, any idea must be put to the test. It may be a non-sense and a deception. It could be that it is a "pretender" and not really "God-given".

How can Abraham be convinced that Isaac, the second-born, is *the* "male" heir and not Ishmael, the first-born? By seeing if he is prepared to sacrifice him?

In chapter 22, God tempts Abraham. He calls Abraham who says, "Behold, here I am".

And God says, "*Take now thy son, thine only son Isaac* . . . (Only son? Because Ishmael is Abram's son, not Abraham's?) . . . *and offer him . . . for a burnt offering . . .*"

Isaac is curious on the way to the mountain as to where the sacrificial "lamb" is but, when the time comes, appears to make no protest at being "bound" and "laid on the altar upon the wood".

Abraham has "faith" in his inspiration . . .

"*And Abraham stretched forth his hand, and took the knife to slay his son.*"

But immediately the story continues:

"*And the angel of the Lord called unto him out of heaven, and said, Abraham, Abraham: and he said, Here am I.*"

NOW; where am I? Not in the remembered past; not in the imagined future.

NOW; *here am I.*

*

"I am".
Who says, "I am"?
I do.
But who am I?
Who is the "I" in "I am"?
I am that "I".
I am I.
Which of the two "I's" am I, the subject or the object?
I can only be sure through the sacrifice of one or the other.
But the sacrificer cannot be the sacrifice.

That which I claim to be mine—even my identity and my life—must be tested to see if it is truly mine. And if it is not, then I must be prepared to sacrifice it . . . otherwise I deceive myself.

I am that "I" which remains when I have had the faith to surrender all that I realise "I" am not.

*

147

This is all something of a conundrum! . . . which requires the mind "to go up into a mountain", as it were, to contemplate the rarified outposts of its assumptions.

The trouble is that "at these heights" words become less and less able to describe the experience.

However, it is worth the attempt for, although it may sound elusive and frustrating pursuing the nature of the "I", no hunt could be more worthwhile.

What is the point of my saying, believing or doing anything if it is not known who is doing it and why?

*

It is perhaps worth pausing to note what some of the main participants in the story say when they first use the word "I" (if at all):

God: ". . . I have given . . ."

Adam: '. . . I heard thy voice . . . I was afraid . . . I was naked . . ."

Eve: ". . . I did eat . . ."

Cain: ". . . I know not: Am I . . ."

(Abel: does not speak).

(Seth: does not speak).

(Noah: speaks but never says "I").

(Shem, Ham, Japheth: do not speak).

Abram: '. . . I know that thou art . . ."

Abraham: '. . . I have found favour . . ."

Isaac: ". . . I said, Lest I die . . ."

*

The Lord's covenant with Abraham begins, "I am the Almighty God . . ."

And later Abraham uses the phrase "I am" himself, after Sarah's death:

And Abraham stood up from before his dead, and spake unto the sons of Heth, saying,

I am a stranger and a sojourner with you: give me a possession of a burying place with you, that I may bury my dead out of my sight.

(Genesis, 23: 3, 4)

Who am I?

Am I a stranger that you know not where I came from at birth nor where I go at death? And a sojourner in that I cannot stay for ever?

"*I am* the Lord thy God . . ."

Whose God?

"*I am* a stranger and a sojourner with you . . . "

With *whom*?

With *me*?

". . . stood up from before his dead . . . that *I* may bury *my* dead out of *my* sight . . ."

Who does the Lord say he is?

"I am . . ."

*

As we focus on these crucial and rarified questions, we have probably gone as far as we usefully can in this pursuit. By now the two alternatives in looking at the Judaic tradition should be apparent . . . at least in the context of this book.

One alternative is that Judaism as a religion can remain as it is ordinarily regarded. That is to say that it is a faith based on an ancient story about the early history of a tribe, reaching back to a fantastical myth as to how the world was created and man began. The religion is conventional in that it pre-supposes an almighty power to which man is subject. This power is variously named and man's fate is governed by his relationship with that power however he may conceive of it—even as vaguely located somewhere "out there" in space. In the case of Judaism, the power's relationship is especially directed at a particular group of humans and is couched primarily in terms of how man should behave according to the laws revealed to certain men in the remote past by the power itself.

The second alternative is that the story, especially as related in the Torah, is a kind of message or comprehensive plan which reveals the laws that govern and give meaning to any human being's life, not as a historical, physical existence, but as descriptive of the mind's experience as it evolves and fulfils itself within the body's lifetime. The characters and their stories represent guidance for the mind as it searches for what it needs to understand.

Thus the performance of the ordinary, mundane religion preserves the story intact; but the secret of its power and persistence, if we accept the second alternative, lies in the fact that that scripture contains within it the most extraordinary and miraculous revelation for each one who is prepared to search for it.

Twelve

One of the keys to making Judaism comprehensible and significant—to us, now—is, as we have suggested, to see that *history reveals* the Law. Whether it be the history of a nation or a tribe, or your *own history*, it will reveal through memory the laws which govern each and every process of life.

And the purpose of that revelation seems to be to enable it to be seen that freedom lies not in trying to change the law or defy it or escape it, but to be free of it through utterly understanding it and obeying it.

*

Thus as far as your own history is concerned, it is no good seeking to change, defy or escape what you have become. It is no good pretending you are what you are not, nor pretending you are not what you are.

It is only through understanding and being obedient to what you are that all the so-called limitations and restrictions inherent within yourself can be transcended. Only in that way can the apparent "evil" in us be transformed—by "growing out of it".

*

So let us be quite clear what we mean by Law.

There are the universal laws of natural process and there are man-made laws, which may or may not be in harmony with the natural laws as they are contrived by man to maintain order within his society in order to ensure its continuity and survival.

This is an important distinction.

The natural law *is* . . . and it inevitably and inexorably governs everything known to man. It encompasses and rules all nature from the smallest atom to the largest star, man himself and all his environment—the temperature, the climate, the seasons, the arable and the arid lands, the sea, the wind, the "life" of every conceivable form.

But such is man's intelligence that he has the power to interfere with natural law and in order to improve his ability to survive, he frequently disrupts the natural processes and balances. All too often he seeks to change, defy or escape the natural law.

From the moment of eating the fruit of the Tree of Knowledge of Good and Evil, man has endeavoured to pursue what he sees as "good" and avoid what he sees as "evil", primarily in relation to pleasure and self-survival.

And the Lord God said, Behold, the man is become as one of us . . .

However, it was knowledge "stolen" at considerable cost—or so it would seem if for the moment we discount the purpose of it.

"God" made sure that imbued with such knowledge we were not to have access to the Tree of Life and we were banished from the Garden of Eden. Thus, "eastward in Eden" we are bound to suffer and die, so long as we presume to try to manipulate the natural law for our own ends in the quest for never-ending life. That is not the way to the Promised Land.

*

Does a plant fear death?

If a man fears death, is it because with the approach of death he will lose his chance of transcending the natural law of destruction and dissolution?

And, if a man does not fear death, may it not well be because he has understood and accepted it?

To transcend (to "rise above" or "climb beyond") the natural law it must first be necessary to know it and then understand it.

And that, it seems, is precisely what the Judaic Law is all about.

The Book of Genesis—also called the First Book of Moses—deals, in detail, with the natural laws which govern our "coming into the world", our becoming what we are, at any moment, physically, mentally and spiritually.

And it is when we come to Abraham, the "father" in each of us, that the "ah" of inspiration is "breathed into us". He represents the possibility of realising the transcendent "I" within.

But it is the fate nevertheless that the line of Abraham has a long way to go, including bondage in Egypt and much suffering, before the wanderings of Exodus and completion of the "historical" cycle.

*

It is the fate of each one of us that we hearken to the "silent voice in the heart"—manifesting as profound questions and the longing for Truth. It is then that we experience "hunger" and seek to transcend the natural progression of event and experience—to "stand back", as it were, to discover what is going on. And it is then that we become well and truly aware of the concepts "good" and "evil". Up to that point we have probably been aware of them in the sense that we have learned the right and wrong of obeying and disobeying the law as presented to us in our formative years. But now they become "real" for us in that we become aware that it is *our responsibility* to *know* and *understand* what the effects are on *us* if we live a good or evil life. It may or may not matter if I disobey man-made law . . . but what if I disobey natural law?

We can continue to obey or disobey man-made law and be appropriately applauded as "good" or condemned as "evil" by our fellow men—but that is as nothing compared with my *really knowing* for myself, in my heart, the worth of my life.

If "conscience" does not trouble us and we are not aware of the responsibility and choice, then we will just allow—or *suffer*—any event or twist of fate to manipulate us, as a plant allows or suffers the passing seasons and the vagaries of weather to dictate its growth and withering.

There is a kind of freedom in this total subjection, this surrender to fate; but there will be no transcendence of it, no "going beyond", no Exodus, only the dissolution of death in the due course of time. And it has nothing to do with the fulfilled freedom available to man.

If the "voice in the heart speaks", it is the "God" within us calling. And that "God" will make us *suffer*—in order that we will search for and come to know the "way out", if we persist in trying to change or defy or escape the natural law instead of "rising above" it.

*

It is given to man—to each of us—to feel the prompting:

"Why should it be this way?" "Why do we suffer and become unhappy?" "Why must I die?" "Why do I want so much that it is denied to me?" "What is the point of life?" "What am I here for?" . . . and so on.

Having eaten of the Tree of Knowledge of Good and Evil, we are *bound* to seek also to eat of the Tree of Life—"to eat and live for ever."

Having been made human, I am already committed to bondage. (And it is fascinating to speculate that, if it is the same "life" in all living things, "I" could easily have been "breathed into" a mouse, or a sparrow, or a blade of grass, instead of this particular body! Why should I be human as opposed to something else?)

The "slavery" comes of knowing the duality of good and evil (Two) whilst sensing or feeling the underlying unity (One) of everything. How can that duality be resolved into understanding the unity?

*

After the triple-son phase from Adam and the triple-son phase from Noah, the conscious "suffering" seems to start when Abram/Abraham has only *two* sons, Ishmael and Isaac.

Although, when Abraham is old and "well stricken with age", he takes another wife, Keturah, by whom he has *six* further sons. Thus, Abram has One son; Abraham has One plus Six, the "magic" or "divine" Seven, thereby introducing that crucial and redeeming number into generation—a number whose power is presaged in the first "archetypes" by Enoch *who walked with God: and he was not; for God took him* and which "sets the scene" for the Messianic prophet foretold by Isaiah, a "saviour" whom the Christians later claimed was Jesus of Nazareth, the seventy-seventh "male" in direct descent from the One, "God" (Luke, 3: 23–28).

*

So Abram/Abraham has two sons—the first a "bastard" and the second "his only son".

There is no identifiable *third* son.

It is as if "I" stand, unrealised, between the "pretender"—the "I" who is the product of my past—and the "I" who will become the legal heir—the future possibility.

Who am I . . . NOW?

The third "son" . . . the third force?

In the dilemma of my maturing into adulthood, when I do not really know who I am nor what I will become, I suffer.

And that suffering is like the "birth pangs" which will give rise to the adult "I" who seems to have three possibilities:

to ignore "God" and exploit the way of the world selfishly—"evil";

to believe in and obey "God" and follow the way of the world selflessly—"good";

to know "God" and forsake the world.

*

And so we could follow our fate according to the historical record of the tribe of Israelites, as it tells of development through the generation of numbers and their relationships to each other and their ultimate dependence on One. And through it we may see the journey of the "I" as the pattern of the "male" and "female" lines interweave through the phases of life.

*

As the history progresses, "prime" numbers appear periodically but they become "weaker" as they recede further and further away from the One. And with the generation of Isaac we enter the Twenties, a phase of Ten governed by Two, the "female".

Isaac marries Rebekah, his second cousin (the grand-daughter of Nahor, Abram's brother) and, once again, she is a barren wife.

But through Isaac's successful plea to God, she eventually conceives and has *twin* sons, Esau and Jacob.

*

And Isaac intreated the Lord for his wife, because she was barren: and the Lord was intreated of him, and Rebekah his wife conceived.

And the children struggled together within her; and she said, If it be so, why am I thus? And she went to inquire of the Lord.

And the Lord said unto her, Two nations are in thy womb, and two manner of people shall be separated from thy bowels; and the one people shall be stronger than the other people; and the elder shall serve the younger.

And when her days to be delivered were fulfilled, behold, there were twins in her womb.

And the first came out red, all over like an hairy garment; and they called his name Esau.

And after that came his brother out, and his hand took hold on Esau's heel; and his name was called Jacob: and Isaac was threescore years old when she bare them.

And the boys grew: and Esau was a cunning hunter, a man of the field; and Jacob was a plain man, dwelling in tents.

And Isaac loved Esau, because he did eat of his venison: but Rebekah loved Jacob.   (Genesis, 26: 21-28)

*

This passage is full of omen for what is to come—due to the duality which even "struggled together within her".

"If it be so, *why am I thus?*"

But it is the "plain man", the younger, who is to overcome and dominate "the cunning hunter", the elder.

Esau ("male", hairy) yields to Jacob ("female", smooth, the second son) and because of "hunger" sells his birthright to the brother "dwelling in tents".

And then, at Rebekah's instigation, Jacob deceives "blind" Isaac and "steals" the blessing of the "father".

The line of generation passes to the "female".

The "emasculated" Esau takes three wives, one a daughter from Ishmael's line.

Thus am "I" drawn into the ways of the world and the One is hidden from sight and ignored.

*

Jacob becomes "rich" by devious means.

And he heard the words of Laban's sons, saying, Jacob hath taken away all that was our father's; and of that which was our father's hath he gotten all this glory.

(Genesis, 31: 1)

*

And Jacob has twelve sons and one daughter.

Two sons by Zilpah, Leah's maid.

Six sons and One daughter (a "false" Seven) by Leah.

Two sons by Bilah, Rachel's maid.

Two sons by Rachel.

These twelve give us the twelve elements ("tribes") which make up the composite character of the whole of humanity (the "Israelites") and the individual psyche also.

*

Jacob has a dream of "the angels of God ascending and descending" a ladder, and the Lord "standing above it" saying, *I am the the Lord God of Abraham thy father, and the God of Isaac: . . .*

Here we see the continuous cycle of the generating outwards and the resolving back to One.

And Jacob makes a condition for his acceptance of God:

And Jacob vowed a vow, saying, If God will be with me, and will keep me in this way that I go, and will give me bread to eat, and raiment to put on,

157

So that I come again to my father's house in peace; then shall the Lord be my God: . . .

(Genesis, 28: 20, 21)

Thus, "I" become separated from the One (God)—by making my belief conditional.

*

Jacob was "left alone"; "and there wrestled a man with him until the breaking of the day".

And he said unto him, What is thy name? And he said, Jacob.

And he said, Thy name shall be called no more Jacob, but Israel: for as a prince hast thou power with God and with men, and hast prevailed.

And Jacob asked him, and said, Tell me, I pray thee, thy name. And he said, Wherefore is it that thou dost ask after my name? And he blessed him there.

(Genesis, 32: 27–29)

Do I not "wrestle" with myself? And do I know the name of my protagonist, who struggles with me in the "darkness" of my mind . .

*

We do not now have space left to go into the significance in detail of the later phases of Genesis . . . and perhaps that is appropriate since we have reached a point in this essay where each must begin to interpret for himself or herself in the light of personal experience.

For we could say that at this point the fate is now "sealed".

As in the history we come to the phase of the long bondage in Egypt, so the human will at this stage in the lifetime . . . or in the present moment . . . becomes totally encompassed or subservient to the ways and demands of the world. The will is surrounded by circumstance—that which "stands round" our potential contribution to the world.

This is taken further in the story by the experience of the "twelve sons" of Israel and in particular, as the "real I", by Joseph, who "dies" in Egypt.

*

And Joseph said unto his brethren, I die; and God will surely visit you, and bring you out of this land unto the land which he sware unto Abraham, to Isaac, and to Jacob.

And Joseph took an oath of the children of Israel, saying, God will surely visit you, and ye shall carry up my bones from hence.

So Joseph died, being an hundred and ten years old: and they embalmed him, and he was put in a coffin in Egypt.

(Genesis, 50: 24–26)

*

God will surely visit you . . .
The oath of the dying Joseph . . .
The Genesis, the coming into being, is over.
The bondage is complete.
It now depends on "God ' . . .
NOW is the Exodus . . . through the inspiration and teaching of Moses, the law-giver.
It is another "book" . . . yet to be "read" . . . by you and me . . . as we suffer in Egypt and search for the "way out".

Thirteen

This book has a beginning.

You could turn to the first page and read:

"This book, as with a religion, has to begin . . . somewhere in place and time."

The Pentateuch has a beginning.

We may turn to its first page and read:

In the beginning God created the heaven and the earth.

Every book comes to an end, as this one will shortly do (although we the authors feel we have scarcely begun to write it yet. It is bewildering how in trying to describe a feeling one always seems to skirt round the edge of it and never really gets to the heart of it!).

You, the reader, may turn to the final page *now* and may read the last words of this last chapter—whatever they may be, for we, at this moment *now*, have not yet got there.

The Pentateuch has an ending; and we may turn to the last page of it and, although it was first written down centuries ago, may *now* read:

And in all the mighty land, and in all the great terror which Moses shewed in the sight of all Israel.

Between the beginning and the ending of any book there are words—the continuing or the content of the book.

To know the content, we have only to read the words.

To read the words, we must first have had the experience of learning the law of letters. Once we learn how words are formed by letters in relation to each other, then we are able to read and sound words. Once we have learned to experience how words are governed in their relationship with each other, then we are able to read and sound sentences. Once we are able to read sentences, then we are able to read the content of the book.

You, the reader, cannot know before the beginning of the book how it came to be created; and you cannot know after its ending what happens after the final full stop.

Likewise with our lives—we cannot know before the beginning of our coming into being and we cannot know after our final dissolution. We can only know the content—the continuing experience of our being here. All we have is our history—in the letters, words and sentences of our existence.

*

Once we have read part of the book, then the first reading of some of the pages is in the past. We may well not remember word for word what we have read—but the book is here now and we can turn back to any page and remind ourselves.

However, as we turn back into the book's "memory", we may find that a particular page of its past *now*, means something different from its meaning when it was first "lived". We will be reading it in the light of our present experience, from the point of view that we have now reached.

NOW . . . always the light of NOW.

In that case, although the book has a manifest ending in place and time, in what sense can it ever be said to be "dead"?

The body begins, continues and ends.

But who is reading its history and what is understood from the experience?

*

The manifest form—the "body" of the book—exists between two letters—the first letter of the first word and the last letter of the last word. There are no words to express before the beginning and after the ending. And before the first and last letters are written, there is only blank paper.

Why else should we have been given the gift of language if not to enable us to *understand* . . . ourselves and the relationships between ourselves and the universe?

The Pentateuch begins with the letter "I" and ends with the letter "L" (in the English language, of course).

In the beginning . . . in the sight of all Israel.

And in between is the content, the ever-present history; in between is the meaning of it all.

But to what degree is the meaning understood?

*

A word or sound expressed means something.

But to what extent is it understood?

It depends on whether the originator knows what is meant to be expressed and whether the recipient has the same degree of experience to understand what is meant.

With nouns standing for physical objects, it is not difficult for us to understand each other if we speak the same learned language. We both more or less understand each other when we say "table".

But when we move into activity and the abstract, it becomes more difficult. And if we become confused, we may try to resolve the difficulty by seeking an official definition, a "neutral third force", say a dictionary. And there we may seek to find the roots of the word, take it apart if composite and thereby discover the parts of which it is composed.

Compose: from Latin *com*, "with", and *pausare*, "to cease, rest, lie or lay down"; confused with and blended in meaning with *ponere*, "to place".

You may compose a piece of prose or a piece of music. And you also may be composed!

"To place with" or "to rest with" . . . Who is composing or being composed?

The dictionary takes us so far . . . but how do we get to the real meaning . . . how do we understand?

*

Once we believe we know what a word means, then we tend to

use it habitually—and rarely pause, "rest", to consider whether we may understand it, "place" it, better.

Just consider the words on this page; they are familiar; we do not have to pause or rest and wonder if we really understand what they mean, whether we have "placed" them accurately as the mind assumes the meaning of them. The trouble is that the words may cease to have precise meaning and may form, instead, a blurred and general meaning as conveyed by the passing sentences.

And the more the letters and words are "passed over" in this way, the greater the possibility that, through the passage of time, the meaning conveyed may change completely.

Take, for example, the word "suffer".

Suffer: from Latin *sub*, "under", and *ferre*, "to bear or carry"; to undergo, to endure, to tolerate, to permit, to experience, be subjected to . . . (transitive); to feel pain or punishment, to sustain loss, to be injured, to be executed or martyred . . . (intransitive).

Suffer.

In the Christian faith religion, Jesus is referred to as "suffering death upon the cross for our redemption . . ." Did he "feel pain" or did he "permit" . . . or both at the same time?

In what sense may the Israelites or Jews be said to have "suffered"?

Above all, who is suffering?

*

And so words are not foolproof. They depend on the degree of understanding of the originator and the recipient.

If we would *understand* Judaism and its Law then, as set down in the scriptures, we must depend on the level of our interpretation . . . which will depend on our desire to understand, our memory and our ability to relate meaning to our experience.

And hence, in understanding how it became composed, we may understand how we may be composed?

*

If we wish we may quite simply approach the scriptures as *history*.

163

We can take them as a series of stories which describe events that happened in sequence through passing time.

History in this sense can never be whole, complete. Today will be tomorrow's history, and tomorrow will be the history of the day after that. History "repeats itself" as it continues on and on towards the end of time, the "ultimate finite".

Certainly it will reveal the Law, and we would do well to learn the lessons of history . . . whether it be the history of mankind or our own personal history.

But that is only the "feminine" half of the story.

"History" derives from Greek, meaning "knowing, learned, wise man, judge".

Being obedient to the revealed Law is the "female" aspect of religion; understanding it is the challenge to the "male" half of the psyche.

*

The end of history can only be the end of time itself.

And this is equally true of each of us individually . . . the personal history of each one of us.

One half of the story is that we learn from experience to obey our fate (for it cannot be changed). The other half is what arises out of that history . . . how we understand and are able to transcend that fate.

*

We are each of us the product of circumstance—from the moment of our individual conception to the moment of our individual death. Before the embodiment and after the disembodiment, there was and will be a blank . . . nothing, as far as my mind is concerned.

Further, until the moment of my death, my story must be incomplete. And after the moment of death, when my story will be complete, I will no longer be embodied. Will I never know the complete story . . . unless it be *in the moment* of death itself?

*

164

The story of my life follows a "horizontal" line, through passing time, from conception to death.

C onceptiongestationbirthadolescencematurityoldagedeat H

The only possible way of making sense out of this continuing line of letters or sounds is to "break it up" and introduce *space*. (Just as the pauses between notes are essential to music, the breaks between words are essential to intelligible speech, and the placing of breaks and vowels into Hebrew consonants gives intelligible meaning to the scriptures.)

And let us remember that it is only passing time (inducing the mechanics of writing as a sequence of letters) that enables us to read along the line and evolve the meaning. Without both space and sequential continuity, our continuous line of letters above would look something like this:

■

Just a black blob which would not tell us very much!

*

So, what are we trying to say in this book!

We have taken certain stories from the Book of Genesis and have put them down in certain space and sequence, and set them in a context of other words. If there is to be inspiration for you, the reader, it must come from the space between the words.

We have related them to certain experience, particularly to discreet phases in the psychological experience of coming to be an individual in the history of a life, in order to see if they mean anything to us NOW, so that we might better understand that life.

But, again, let us state and be quite clear—if for you, the reader, the history and the laws of commandment are sufficient, then this book—and all others like it—may be put aside.

It is simply a question of how you view religion—as something to be ignored, or obeyed, or understood.

*

When we speak of the stories meaning something other than

historical record, we are entering a new dimension. For we "stand back" from being involved . . . just as we may "stand back" from being involved in making our daily history . . . in order to see what it is meaning. And in standing back we come into the present, for the meaning of a religion, or of ourselves, is not revealed in the past. It is then not history; it is NOW.

Every memory of our own past—even if it was only a minute ago—can only *mean* something if we recall it to mean something NOW.

Mean (singular), means (plural): derived from Latin, "mid", "middle"; condition, quality, course, equally removed from two opposite (usually blamable) extremes, *term between first and last terms of a mathematical progression*, that by which result is brought about, pecuniary resources, in every possible way, second of three quantities of which the first is to it as it is to the third, inferior or poor understanding, ignoble, small-minded, secretly ashamed, purpose, have in mind, design towards an objective, intend to convey or indicate a sense, be of importance to another, signify, import . . .

How well do we know what "mean" means?

What do "I" mean?

What do I mean to myself?

*

Can I be anywhere . . . any *where* at all?

Can I lose myself . . . and say, "Where am I"?

The country around me may not be familiar, and that may prompt me to say, "Where am I?" But, in all honesty, I know where I am, don't I? I am *here* . . . surrounded by unfamiliar country. And if I cannot name the country, then I may call it "nowhere".

But I am here, in nowhere.

I am *now-here*.

I am always *here-now*; there is *now-here* else that I can be!

Is this all an irritating game with words?

Perhaps.

But it is so crucial that we should understand NOW . . . for there is no other time or place to do it.

166

NOW, I am "creating" every facet of my experience—my past, my future, my present, my seeing and hearing, and tasting, and touching and smelling—all is created or re-created here and now, through the experience of this body and mind.

NOW is the moment of creation.

Re-created past and projected future are illusory.

Consider it. Why not? At this moment, as *you* are reading these words . . . NOW is the reality . . . what you are sensing, what you are feeling, what you are thinking, is being created NOW.

*

"No!" the chronological, logical, sequential, part of the mind will object. (Let us call that "half" of the mind, the "female" half— "Eve"). "For there to be creation there must first be a conception, and then a gestation, and then a birth. Time can be remembered . . ."

"All right," counters Adam (the "male" half), "that may *explain* how you came to be here to satisfy desire for logical continuity through time but how is it relevant to being here now? What reality is there in believing you were once something that you now are not? Do you want to be dependent on memory? Or what reality is there in believing you are going to become something that now you are not? Do you want to be dependent on dreams?"

And Eve could reply, "In me is the material which governs your potential—according to my past. And hence it governs what you may become—your future possibilities."

"Very good," concedes Adam. "But, nevertheless, your functioning is now. Now you remember; now you imagine; now is the real moment."

"What moment?"

"The moment for living, for being, for understanding. What price existing in the past? You are dead! What price existing in the future? You are not yet born. Now, you must die; now, you must be reborn. Now is the time of moment; the only existence is now; the only living experience is now. Give up your memories and your dreams!"

But Eve counters, "But being here now depends on my body.

167

For if my body had not formed and matured in time, how would you know you are here? Then where are you? You depend on my body to contain and sustain you. Without my body, you could not exist at all."

"I grant you that," says Adam, "but what is the point of your body if I am not in it? Your history and your future possibilities are as nothing if I AM not here. How else will they be known, if I am not here to witness them?"

So might the dialogue continue . . .

Eve, for ever the sustaining complement of Adam—providing "she" does not wander off on sentimental journeys into the past or unrealistic dreams of the future! Providing she is obedient to NOW, "she" is the essential partner of Adam, without whom "he" would not know himself to exist.

*

Is this not so?

Is not the past memory and the future dream only relevant in the light of NOW?

If in your past you lost, say, a limb, then you will be without a limb. The past experience will bring a direct legacy to the present experience. But is not the experience NOW that you are without a limb? And is it not your memory that suggests that it was not always the case? And, further, is it not your memory NOW that makes you *regret* NOW that you lost the limb *then*? And may not the regret make you suffer? What is going on? You are suffering NOW because of the result of an event in the *past*?

But if "creation" is NOW—the continual "in the beginning"—and every moment is a spontaneous re-creation of the world . . . then NOW the limbless are created limbless; NOW, it is neither "good" nor "evil"; it simply IS.

For such a statement to be a living reality in us, it is necessary that we should discipline and transcend the habitual *thinking* of the mind, bound as it is to the chain (or in some traditions, the "wheel") of continuity, repetition and perpetuation in passing time, so that there is connection with the everlasting and present One-ness. We may only become free and whole through obedience to the Law of One—the Lord is One.

*

For the lips of a strange woman drop as an honeycomb, and her mouth is smoother than oil:
But her end is bitter as wormwood, sharp as a twoedged sword.
Her feet go down to death; her steps take hold on hell.
Lest thou shouldest ponder the path of life, her ways are moveable, that thou canst not know them.
Hear me now therefore, O ye children, and depart not from the words of my mouth.
Remove thy way far from her, and come not nigh the door of her house:
Lest thou give thine honour unto others, and thy years unto the cruel:
Lest strangers be filled with thy wealth; and thy labours be in the house of a stranger;
And thou mourn at the last, when thy flesh and thy body are consumed,
And say, How have I hated instruction, and my heart despised reproof;
And have not obeyed the voice of my teachers, nor inclined mine ear to them that instructed me!

(Proverbs, 5: 3–13)

*

When the Jew says (in "The Shema") "The Lord is One," he is reminding himself of the one that not only gave rise to all "numbers" from the beginning, but which is *in* every "number" . . . as the "I" is present in every moment of my existence.

The acknowledgement of, and then the longing for, unification—the realisation of the real "I"—is the cornerstone of Judaism and of all religion ("binding back"). It represents the only "way out" of the multiplicity, duality, ignorance and confusion of life.

We have suggested, in this book, that as far as we have traced through Genesis, we have seen the structure of the Law of our coming into mature adulthood. And as the code of numbers—stemming inevitably from One—proliferates, so the children of Israel "multiply" and "matter" becomes more dense and more complex, subject to increasing numbers of subsidiary laws (as in the Books of Numbers and Leviticus).

And we have suggested that the "I"—the real identity—is eventually "sold into Egypt" as the demands of the world encompass on all sides and the emphasis is placed on involvement and physical survival.

And, further, that the "way out" depends on Moses.

*

Moses is born at a time of adversity for not only are the Israelites in bondage in Egypt but Pharoah has ordered that every Hebrew son that is born "shall be cast into the river".

Unlike the generations in Genesis, the names of the father and mother of Moses are not given (and neither does he marry). We are simply told that "a man of the house of Levi . . . took to wife a daughter of Levi". (Is it purely coincidence that "Levi" is an anagram of both "live" and "evil"?).

Such is the threat to Moses as a "male" son, that he is "hidden" for three months and then, when his mother can no longer keep him, he is concealed in an "ark" on the "river's brink".

Strangely, Moses is found, and then adopted as her "son", by, of all people, Pharoah's daughter, an act which must have been in direct defiance of her father's command.

*

The more demands and restrictions the world places on us, the more desperately the questions are likely to arise in us. We have long since left the "land of our nativity" and we do not know the "father" and "mother" of the individuality that lies "hidden" within our minds. But as it grows and we are guided by the religious law it has the "ark" of the ancient covenant as its protection.

The analogy may be followed in detail if it is within our experience

and we have a mind to do so but one important principle emerges
—the nature of the "I" of Exodus.

We may decide to set out to leave what we feel to be our bondage
in order to find our individuality . . . but we need help.

It is "God" who speaks to Moses in an enigmatic verse of chapter
3 of Exodus, after the angel of the Lord has appeared "in a flame
of fire out of the midst of a bush".

*And when the Lord saw that he turned aside to see, God called unto
him out of the midst of the bush, and said, Moses, Moses. And he
said, Here am I.* (Verse 4).

Moses *turned aside to see* . . . God called his name . . . *Here am I.*

And after telling Moses that he is to "bring forth" the children
out of Egypt, Moses says:

*. . . Behold, when I come unto the children of Israel, and shall say
unto them, The God of your fathers hath sent me unto you; and they
shall say to me, What is his name? What shall I say unto them?*

*And God said unto Moses, I AM THAT I AM: and he said, Thus
shalt thou say unto the children of Israel, I AM hath sent me unto you.*

(Exodus, 3: 13, 14)

*

What a strange proclamation . . . and yet . . . what a magnificent
and challenging reminder to the confused and bewildered mind:

I AM THAT I AM . . .

I AM hath sent me unto you . . .

*

With that "call to freedom", we may begin the exodus.

But as the story continues there is much difficulty, doubt and
trouble ahead. And this is where Moses takes on his crucial role as
leader and lawgiver, for what is required now is discipline and
obedience—whether it be the discipline of the obedience to religious
doctrine, or obedience to one's better judgement and the discipline
applied to oneself—self-discipline.

*

The most celebrated of the Laws given to Moses are of course the Ten Commandments, the decalogue, spoken by God on Mount Sinai.

The Lord is One . . . his commandments are Ten.

*

And God spake all these words, saying,

I am the Lord thy God, which have brought thee out of the land of Egypt, out of the house of bondage.

Thou shalt have no other gods before me.

Thou shalt not make unto thee any graven image, or any likeness of any thing that is in heaven above, or that is in the earth beneath, or that is in the water under the earth:

Thou shalt not bow down thyself to them, nor serve them: for I the Lord thy God am a jealous God, visiting the iniquity of the fathers upon the children unto the third and fourth generation of them that hate me;

And shewing mercy unto thousands of them that love me, and keep my commandments.

Thou shalt not take the name of the Lord thy God in vain; for the Lord will not hold him guiltless that taketh his name in vain.

Remember the sabbath day, to keep it holy.

Six days shalt thou labour, and do all thy work:

But the seventh day is the sabbath of the Lord thy God: in it thou shalt not do any work, thou, nor thy son, nor thy daughter, thy man-servant, nor thy maidservant, nor thy cattle, nor thy stranger that is within thy gates:

For in six days the Lord made heaven and earth, the sea, and all that in them is, and rested the seventh day: wherefore the Lord blessed the sabbath day, and hallowed it.

Honour thy father and thy mother: that thy days may be long upon the land which the Lord thy God giveth thee.

Thou shalt not kill.

Thou shalt not commit adultery.

Thou shalt not steal.

Thou shalt not bear false witness against thy neighbour.

Thou shalt not covet thy neighbour's house, thou shalt not covet thy neighbour's wife, nor his manservant, nor his maidservant, nor his ox, nor his ass, nor anything that is thy neighbour's.

(Exodus, 20: 1–17)

*

These commandments are not of course exclusive to Judaism. They are essential to every man "born of Adam".

On the one hand they spring out of man's desire to survive and on the other from his desire for purity and perfection—the "descent" and the "ascent" of the "ladder", as it were.

We may simply take them as a list of ten items, like a laundry list, or we can look for more subtle aspects of their composition.

*

For example, we may see the Ten as One and three triads or trinities of Three (from which all numbers emerge, as do all laws).

Not coveting, nor bearing false witness, not stealing—the disciplinary basis of the order, purity and survival within society.

Not committing adultery, not killing, honouring parents—the disciplinary basis of the order, purity and survival of the society itself, tribal or racial.

Keeping the holiness of the sabbath, not taking the Lord's name in vain, not making graven images—the disciplinary basis for the order, purity and survival of the religious tradition and spiritual life.

And above all, "in the beginning", that upon which it all depends, the omnipotence of the One, the Lord God.

*

From the point of view of the Law "descending", coming down to us as mortals on earth, or from the point of view of we mortals down here looking up to the Law "ascending", the dispensation begins or ends in a tripartite statement—a trinity of verses:

God spake (1st verse) . . . I am the Lord thy God (2nd verse) . . .

Thou shalt have no other gods (3rd verse). We could say that these represent the One in its threefold aspect—conditioning, active, passive.

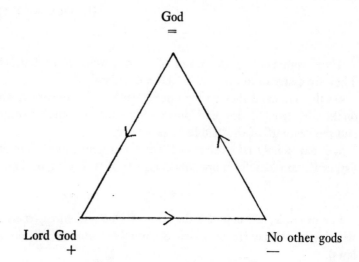

(And it seems probable that if we looked carefully we would see significance in the different expressions used throughout the text —God, Lord thy God, Lord, and so on.)

*

As we look "upwards" towards "God" and aspire towards perfection . . . as we are raised by the Law, as it were . . . we may also see the commandments as a "ladder" of mind discipline:

1. Not coveting . . . not desiring that which is not one's own, to be other than what one really is;
2. Not bearing false witness . . . not speaking through a "false I" but speaking honestly;
3. Not stealing . . . not taking that which is not one's own, not adding unlawfully to oneself;
4. Not committing adultery . . . not desiring to be other than true to oneself;

5. Not killing . . . not eliminating that which threatens oneself;
6. Honouring parents . . . acknowledgement of that which enabled oneself to be;
7. Keeping the sabbath . . . remembering the holiness or wholeness of the One;
8. Not taking the name in vain . . . not speaking of the One as anything less than Absolute;
9. Not making any graven image . . . not imagining there to be any other than the One;
10. "I am the Lord thy God . . . Thou shalt have no other gods" . . . One *is*; alone, all-one; atonement . . . there is nought else; nothing else that is real or true.

*

It is presumably our conditioning in passing time that persuades us to look for sequence in one direction—just as we read the language of this writing from left to right. How does it come about that another language—Hebrew, for example—is written from right to left?

We have said that today will be tomorrow's history and that tomorrow will be the history of the day after that.

For a moment we may glimpse . . . the future is the past coming towards us.

We tend to think of ourselves moving from the past into the future; but really is it not that the future is moving into and becoming the past? We think we are going one way; but which way is time going? Back towards the beginning?

Are we going towards death or is death coming towards us?

We are used to moving what we think is forwards; but could it be an illusion—as when you sit in a stationary train and another train passes in the opposite direction to the one you are facing and you then feel that your train is moving forwards?

Identified with the physical body, it appears that I move through time; but if I "stand back" and consider, then it seems that it is time that is passing—from future into past.

What is going on?

Where is the reality?

Supposing that the *future* Promised Land is a "mirage" continually receding as we think we are moving towards it? Supposing that it is an illusion to believe that we can ever get there, in time?

Supposing that in reality it is here, NOW?

*

Supposing that the moment of our death is "fixed" in time—that our days are literally numbered?

Would we then concern ourselves with pretending that it will not come, or worry about its approach, or attempt to postpone it? Would we not surrender our obsession with increased longevity? Would we not perhaps prepare for it instead?

*

For as long as we search in the future for our Promised Land or in the past for our Eden, we will suffer the ever-projecting and ever-receding generation and degeneration of the finite.

*

Then a cloud covered the tent of the congregation, and the glory of the Lord filled the tabernacle.

And Moses was not able to enter into the tent of the congregation because the cloud abode thereon, and the glory of the Lord filled the tabernacle.

And when the cloud was taken up from over the tabernacle, the children of Israel went onward in all their journeys:

But if the cloud were not taken up, then they journeyed not till the day that it was taken up.

For the cloud of the Lord was upon the tabernacle by day, and fire was on it by night, in the sight of all the house of Israel, throughout all their journeys.

(The final five verses of the Book of Exodus).

*

Moses is permitted to see but is not allowed to go into the land which the Lord gave to the children of Israel—because he "trespassed" . . . because he failed to sanctify the Lord *in the midst of the children of Israel.*

Moses the lawgiver, who guides the tribe to the very threshold of the Promised Land, dies; and as he passes the responsibility of leadership to Joshua, the son of Nun, the Pentateuch comes to an end.

The teaching of the Law is over. The discipline has gone as far as it can go.

In this culmination, we may see the end of wilfulness, the "death of the ego". For even that "I" which propounds the Law, exerts the discipline and prepares the way to lead the mind out of its bondage of ignorance is not "fit" to "cross over Jordan". No matter how noble, how good, how religious . . . man cannot by his own efforts alone redeem his life.

The river Jordan represents another quantum jump . . . the ultimate realisation wherein there is no death . . . a realisation that may only be brought about by divine intervention.

But that is not, as it were, in the passing time of "journeys"; only when "the glory of the Lord" fills "the tabernacle".

*

However we may each of us come to understand this "mystical" experience, we may learn through the Judaic Law how to prepare for it.

To be reunited with the One, to realise the real "I", we may learn from the Law revealed by history. And that possibility is always NOW. We have become through fate what we are NOW. And what we may become is not an imagined projection in the future—for that future will then be our past—but will depend on how we transform the future NOW.

If our deepest question is, "Who am I?", then the answer will not be revealed by looking along the line of passing time, either in the past or in the future.

We cannot grow physically younger. Having left the womb, we cannot go back to it.

Nor, having lost our innocence, can we regain it.

Nor can we avoid the approaching death of the body.

The only possibility of "redemption" is to make a "perpendicular" connection "upwards" from the "horizontal" line of passing time in the moment NOW.

Here I stand NOW.

The past stretches behind me, receding into the mists of finite time, never reaching a known beginning. The future is ever coming towards me, passes me, and runs like a river back into those same mists. (Perhaps somewhere, the distant past becomes the distant future, completing a cycle out in the eternal darkness.)

But I stand here and now, reaching up towards the "motionless centre", longing for that One which originates and contains All.

*

To every thing there is a season, and a time to every purpose under the heaven:

A time to be born, and a time to die; a time to plant, and a time to pluck up that which is planted;

A time to kill, and a time to heal; a time to break down, and a time to build up;

A time to weep, and a time to laugh; a time to mourn, and a time to dance;

A time to cast away stones, and a time to gather stones together; a time to embrace, and a time to refrain from embracing;

A time to get, and a time to lose; a time to keep, and a time to cast away;

A time to rend, and a time to sew; a time to keep silence, and a time to speak;

A time to love, and a time to hate; a time of war, and a time of peace.

What profit hath he that worketh in that wherein he laboureth?

I have seen the travail, which God hath given to the sons of men to be exercised in it.

He hath made every thing beautiful in his time: also he hath set the world in their heart, so that no man can find out the work that God maketh from the beginning to the end.

I know that there is no good in them, but for a man to rejoice, and to do good in his life.

And also that every man should eat and drink, and enjoy the good of all his labour, it is the gift of God.

I know that, whatsoever God doeth, it shall be for ever: nothing can be put to it, nor any thing taken from it: and God doeth it, that men should fear before him.

That which hath been is now; and that which is to be hath already been; and God requireth that which is past.

(Ecclesiastes, 3: 1–15)

*

In the beginning God created the heaven and the earth . . .

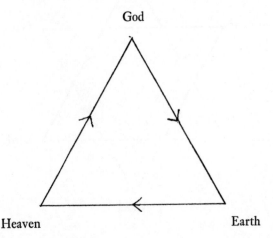

God

Heaven   Earth

That which hath been is now; and that which is to be hath already been; and God requireth that which is past.

Hear, O Israel: The Lord our God, the Lord is One!

179

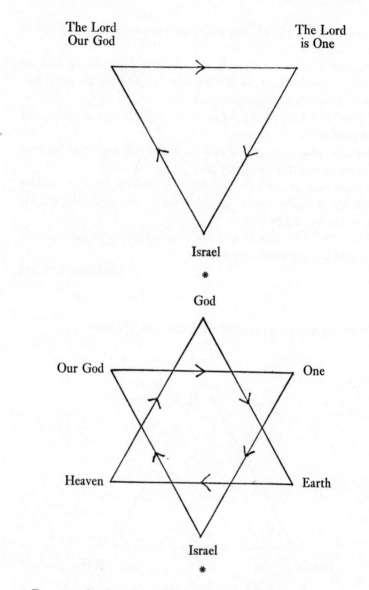

Between the first line of Genesis and the first line of the Shema lies a vast gulf—as deep and as wide as the mind.
Who is God?

and
Who am I?

*

God *and* I?
Who created who?
One + One = Two
If that duality were resolved, who would remain?
One × One = One
One ÷ One = One
One − One = Nothing

*

The illusory duality of God (or no God) *and* I will not be resolved
by persisting in ignorance or believing in separation.

One or other will suffer.

And God will not be proved to exist elsewhere by the intellect's
theories and analyses. Which One would be proved?

Only by total sacrifice of all that I think I am will it be resolved ...

*And Enoch walked with God: and he was not; for God took
him.*

Such surrender requires an unconditional following of the
longing of the heart and may only be accomplished by utter faith
... for there will be Nothing left.

It is only Love that can reunite and realise the reality of One.

And such Love is not the cosy warmth of "togetherness"; it is
the overwhelming vocation to be One through the sacrifice of all
else.

Love is sacrifice ... the making holy ... the making whole.

*Love ye therefore the stranger: for ye were strangers in the land of
Egypt.* (Deuteronomy, 10: 19).

The Judaic Law clearly defines what we have become through
Genesis ... and what we must give up through Exodus.

And that includes even our identity and exclusivity ... our
very "Jewishness".

*

Set me as a seal upon thine heart, as a seal upon thine arm: for love is strong as death; jealousy is cruel as the grave: the coals thereof are coals of fire, which hath a most vehement flame.

(The Song of Solomon, 8: 6)

THE SEAL OF SOLOMON

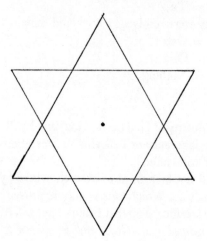